# Dynamic Discovery

## A Process of Self Evaluation

### By George Bissett

Copyright ©2015 George Bissett.

All rights reserved. No part of this work may be reproduced or transmitted in any form or by any means – graphic, electronic or mechanic, including photocopying, recording, taping or information storage and retrieval systems – without the prior written permission of the publisher.

In other words, PLEASE don't steal our stuff. We worked hard to prepare it. Plus, the Dynamic Discovery program is all about honesty ... and stealing is just wrong.

LIMITS OF LIABILITY/DISCLAIMER OF WARRANTY

This material is designed for educational purposes only. The author takes no responsibility for any misappropriation of the contents stated in this e-book and thus cannot and will not be held liable for any damages incurred because of it. While the author of this book has made utmost efforts to obtain updated and accurate information contained herein, the author and/or the publisher of the book cannot be held liable for any damage or loss caused by the content of this book. The author of the book does not warranty the accuracy of the contents and disclaims all warranties with respect to the information contained herein, its accuracy and applications. The advice presented in this book may not be suitable for everyone. The information contained herein is not intended to substitute for informed medical advice or training. This book is not a substitute for professional advice and the information in this e-book should not be used to diagnose or treat a health problem. Dynamic Discovery is a process of self-evaluation. Neither the author nor the publisher of this book is engaged in rendering any professional services. If expert assistance and guidance is needed, professional help should be sought.

The author of the e-book does not endorse any person whose quotations have been used in this book. Neither the author nor the publisher of the book takes any credit for the cited quotations. Individual results may vary.

# ACKNOWLEDGMENTS

Writing this book has provided me with both pleasure and frustration: pleasure because I had long ago written out a poorly formatted and incomplete document that I used as a guide for several of my workshops; frustration because I had trouble expressing in writing what seemed so clear in my head. And then five people entered my life and things began to happen.

The first two people are Bob and Dawn Bray, who became good friends and a sounding board for my many rants and also provided me with excellent feedback. Check out our website (www.dynamicdiscovery.ca) and you will see that Bob has excellent 'helping' skills of his own.

Then I contacted Lise Merle, who had previously done some inventive consulting work for me, and told her what I was hoping to do. She provided the layout for this book. Her contributions are gratefully appreciated.

Natasha Burkholder (http://littlebcreative.com) designed all of the graphics used throughout the book – from the cover all the way to the end.

And last, but far from least, is Christina (Chrissy) Rice who has converted the book into the various formats and has looked after publishing issues, all social media and other marketing chores: find her at www.completeadminsolutions.ca

PLEASE NOTE THAT A WORKBOOK IS AVAILABLE TO ACCOMPANY THIS BOOK.

CHECK FOR INFORMATION AT
WWW.DYNAMICDISCOVERY.CA.

# Table Of Contents

Preface ................................................................. i
Part 1 – How The Mind Works ............................. 1
Why Your Mind Can Work Against You ................ 6
The Human Mind .................................................. 18
Control Car Theory ............................................... 20
Control Computer Theory .................................... 22
Our Basic Human Needs ...................................... 28
Knowing What We Want ...................................... 34
Using The Past To Create Change ...................... 38
Part 2 ..................................................................... 39
Control Theory ...................................................... 42
Introductions ......................................................... 54
Feelings ................................................................. 62
Thinking ................................................................. 70
Doing ..................................................................... 78
Control Car ............................................................ 86
How Relationships Are Affected By Behaviors ..... 92
Relationships As Affected By Needs .................. 100
Solutions .............................................................. 110
Conclusion ........................................................... 119

# LIST OF FIGURES

Figure 1 - How The Mind Works ........................... 7

Figure 2 - The Conscious And Subconscious Mind ................................................................. 18

Figure 3 - A Balanced Example ......................... 20

Figure 4 - An Unbalanced Example .................... 21

Figure 5 - Control Computer ............................. 24

Table 1 - Behavior Examples ............................. 45

Table 2 - Troubling Feelings .............................. 62

Table 3 - Feelings You'd Like To Feel More Of ..... 68

Table 4 - Wanted Thoughts ............................... 76

Table 5 - Unwanted Behaviors .......................... 79

Table 6 - Want To Be Doing ............................... 83

Table 7 - Working List ....................................... 84

Figure 6 - Control Car ....................................... 87

Figure 7 - Overthinking Control Car .................. 89

Figure 8 - Typical Relationship Chart ................ 92

Figure 9 - How An Alcoholic's Needs Are Met ...... 94

Figure 10 - Relationship Chart – Example 1 ....... 97

Figure 11 - Relationship Chart – Example 2 ....... 98

Figure 12 - Your Relationship Chart .................. 99

Figure 13 - Needs Chart ................................... 101

Figure 14 - Your Needs Chart ........................... 102

Figure 15 – Overeater's Needs Chart ................ 104

Figure 16 - How Relationships Meet Needs – Example 1 ...................................................... 106

Figure 17 - How Relationships Meet Needs – Example 2 ...................................................... 108

Figure 18 and Figure 19 - Perspective .............. 121

DYNAMIC DISCOVERY BOOK

## PREFACE

I owe a debt of gratitude to my friend and business partner, Bob Bray, who encouraged me to describe in writing the process that comprised a workshop I created called Dynamic Discovery. It was Bob's advice and support that inspired me to create this book.

Much of the information contained herein is from a summary manual titled 'About Being Human' that I assembled in 1998. I used that manual as my reference resource for counseling sessions, workshop/seminar presentations, and my newsletter entitled 'News & Views'.

At the time that I was committing these words and ideas to paper, I was working as a counselor and program manager for a company called Human Resources Services Ltd. (HRS) – an Employee and Family Assistance Program (EFAP) provider. HRS contracts with various private and public organizations to provide counseling services for their employees. EFAPs act as a bridge between troubled employees (and/or their immediate family members) and the professional resources to help them deal with their problems.

We live in a rapidly changing world which, although fascinating, causes problems and creates troubled people. A good EFAP provider, like HRS, becomes an

i

expert at stress detoxification through dealing with troubled people – most of whom are looking for 'motivation'.

Motivation is a very personal concept, and most so-called motivational programs are largely short-term 'pumps'. Yet the self-improvement and personal development industry has been exploding for more than 25 years (witness the continuing popularity of Tony Robbins and all others of his ilk). There appears to be no slowing down as more and more people are looking for ways to achieve more, or to simply make changes in their lives. In the same vein, the EFAP field is one of the faster growing industries in North America, simply because more employers are coming to understand that EFAPs actually save them money while contributing to workplace efficiency and harmony. The HRS programs were developed to provide education and training to troubled employees and their families, which makes them topical to the problems being encountered today.

Everything these days comes with some kind of a manual – a warranty or guarantee manual, a servicing manual, or an owner's manual – that is, except for us humans! Toasters, cars and TVs all have complete and illustrated instructions, but people are left to guess how to fix human problems or adjust human behaviors.

Does this make any sense? Who on earth gets into more trouble and needs help more often than humans? Some so-called 'experts' say that most of us live a dysfunctional lifestyle – meaning if we were machines, most of us would be recalled. What a depressing thought.

But if you want to discover a different and effective way to make the changes in your life that will lead you to happiness, here is some great news: this book is for you. Within these pages you will find simple and effective ways to create solutions for you.

Throughout my career, I've learned and practiced a number of 'therapy' models that are based upon blaming all of our problems on our upbringing on the care, or lack thereof, provided by parents during childhood. Like this:

"I am a 50-year-old alcoholic. This is probably because my mother set me backwards on the potty and this explains why I've been doing things backwards ever since! Or maybe it was because my parents paid more attention to my sister. In any case, it's not my fault!"

Someone else is to blame. Always. How ludicrous is that?

I have noticed that many people – both male and female – who are experiencing long-term behavioral problems often trace their problems to incidents

involving something a parent did or said that was so significant or traumatic to them at that time of their life that their very personality was altered.

In most cases, the incidents involved the mother. Although this seems on the surface like a major indictment of motherhood, there is an explanation: mothers are usually the primary caregivers during the essential formative years of childhood. Mothers generally have great concern for the safety and well-being of their kids, and often they try to protect them through control and guilt.

Sometimes parents live through their kids, pushing them toward goals and achievements they dreamed of for themselves. This is not to say that most parents deliberately set out to ruin the lives of their children. In fact, most parents want more for their kids than they themselves had. And, not surprisingly, most parents have a very fixed idea of what they want their kids to be and do – regardless of what the kids want.

Our fears and concerns often get projected onto our kids. We think because they are our kids, they must want what we want for them. And if they disappoint us, it must be because they don't understand how much we as parents have invested in them emotionally. "If they really loved me (or us), they would do whatever it took to make me (or us) proud." Therefore, the application of sufficient guilt and other punishment is often called for.

Concern, caring, and protectiveness (called love) on the part of the parent(s), can result in damaging a child's psyche and are often powerful enough to cause them severe behavior problems for many years – maybe even forever.

What is to be done about it? Outlaw parents? Raise kids in government-run communes? Or should we teach people to take responsibility for their own actions, regardless of the hand they were dealt in life?

Let that sink in ...

What? Be responsible for our own actions, even when there is someone else to blame?

Why not? Perhaps if we learned to act according to our own best interest, we wouldn't keep suffering from crippling guilt, anxiety, or inferiority – or try to drink, drug or excessively eat our problems away.

Maybe if we took responsibility for our own thoughts and actions, we could learn to feel better about our own lives, and about ourselves.

But who is going to teach us? By the time most of us become aware that our compensating behaviors aren't working, we're generally parents ourselves, and we may have had one or more intimate relationships that have been destroyed because of our inappropriate or ineffective behaviors.

It is at this point where responsibility for one's self comes into it. This is where we get to pick our own direction and discover what and who we want to be – and Dynamic Discovery will show you, step by step, how to do just that.

To proceed: do what you want, as long as what you want isn't deliberately hurtful or harmful to either yourself or anyone else. This is because you will always experience what you create.

Life is about relationships with people, places and things. The quality of those relationships, whether good or bad, is 100% dependent on how we act – and how we act depends on our Values and Beliefs. This is why sometimes we find ourselves at odds with those around us, and explains why sometimes we engage in conflict or feel out of step with the rest of society. If you're feeling a distance with the people around you – whether you have withdrawn or they have withdrawn – the surest way to bring people closer may be to change your own behavior.

You might ask "Why should I be the one to change?" The answer is "Because you don't like what's happening – so you can change how you feel about it."

'Best interest' means doing things that aren't deliberately hurtful or harmful to either yourself or anyone else.

# DYNAMIC DISCOVERY BOOK

We humans operate with a built-in 'smart system' that's capable of evaluating our needs and determining what to do in order to meet those needs. Once we build our library of activities and events that will help us meet our needs, our 'smart system' will evaluate and choose the best option(s) for us as individuals.

Because no other person can possibly live our lives for us, your 'smart system' dictates that you are the only person on the planet who can make the changes you need to make in order to get what you really, really want – happiness. You are the only one who can restore your own dignity and self-respect. No one else can do that for you.

Let that sink in ...

You are the only one who can do what has to be done to make yourself happy. Nobody else. You. And you can do it. Dynamic Discovery will show you how to do that – and many other things as well.

Recovery is a process that is often filled with moments of sharp, clear insights, and sometimes blazing realizations – but for the most part, recovery is learning to live life from a new and different point of view. Although we've all developed skills and techniques that we use in an attempt to deal with life, if those skills and techniques leave us feeling that something is amiss, the Dynamic Discovery challenge for us is to be open to learning new skills

## GEORGE BISSETT

and to experimenting with different points of view in new and creative ways.

And remember: the human being is the only creature on earth that is not a prisoner of its programming but the master of it. Therefore, none of us needs to live even a minute longer as we are, because we have been endowed with the ability to change ourselves.

Please note there is a workbook available to accompany this book. Check for information at www.dynamicdiscovery.ca

# Part 1 – How The Mind Works

This brief description of how the mind works is inserted at the beginning of Dynamic Discovery for very good reason. Once you know how you think, and why you think the way you do, it is possible to change the way you think.

Let that sink in ...

Only if you know how and why you think the way you do can you change how and what you think.

You might be asking "Why would I want to change the way I think?" and the simple answer is this: if you're not getting what you want from your own life, then you'll have to change what you're doing. As Albert Einstein said, "Insanity: doing the same thing over and over again and expecting different results."

If you want to change anything, you absolutely must do something different. It doesn't matter whether the change is to a human behavior or a recipe for pound cake. Doing something different will produce a change to the outcome. Consider this: if you're an angry person and drive people away, but you don't like being isolated and/or lonely, the answer is to change or to do something different so the outcome is that people aren't driven away anymore.

This is what Dynamic Discovery is all about.

However, before we go any further, it's important for you, the reader, to know that all human problems have simple solutions. Not necessarily easy. Just simple. To clarify, 'simple' means 'not complex'.

For example, let's say that your relationship with food isn't a healthy one. The simple solution is to stop eating so much. Every food abuser has heard this same advice many times, and has rejected it many times. Why would people who overeat reject the right answer? They reject it because it doesn't tell them 'how' to stop overeating. And the 'how' is seldom easy. There will be discomfort and there may even be pain when undertaking change.

In the case of any addiction or obsession, the pain and discomfort in continuing the behavior is known, whereas the pain and discomfort in getting 'clean' is completely unknown. It often appears easier to stick with what we know, but once we understand the pain and/or punishment attached to a decision, it will be easier to do. Half the battle is being able to take the punishment, work through the discomfort, and push back against the pain.

An extreme example would be that of a battered spouse. We are often surprised that a battered woman would ever stay in a relationship with her abuser. And after she finds the courage to leave,

we're downright shocked when she decides to return to the relationship.

It all boils down to this: she stays and/or leaves and returns (sometimes over and over) because she fears the unknown more than she fears the abuse she knows. She knows what life is like with her abuser, and she might believe that tomorrow the abuser will change and they'll have a wonderful life together.

Or she may believe that if she just cares more, does more, or becomes 'better', her abuser won't beat her anymore. Maybe she believes she is as stupid, ugly, and lazy as she's been told, and maybe she can't survive without him. If she does leave him, what will she wind up with? Will she find herself in an even worse situation? Each question, each scenario, takes her into the unknown future where all of her fears reside.

Another example relates to addictions. Most addicts will clean up for a while and then go back to using their drug of choice because they know more about being high or intoxicated than they know about getting and staying clean.

The drunk drinks for confidence, or to relax, or to dance better, or to be funny, or because…

And even when alcohol no longer produces the effect that it once did, the alcoholic thinks, "Maybe tomorrow it will be different! Maybe if I switch from

beer to whiskey or from whiskey to rum or from rum to vodka, it will work again."

The same thing applies for any obsession, of which addictions are just one example.

Every addict uses a substance or behavior to change the circumstances of their life. But merely the thought of being without the substance or behavior is an entry into the unknown. Being clean and/or sober is very scary; because the addict is convinced they need their substance or behavior to cope with the world.

There's a lot of pain and discomfort in the examples above, and fear of an unknown future is a very strong one. We as humans fear what we do not know. This fear is compounded when the human mind gets busy creating ridiculous scenarios of what might happen when we contemplate doing something different.

For example, if someone has collection agents chasing them, every time there's a knock on the door or every time the phone rings, that person's mind will say, "It's the creditors again!" The mind will conjure up all kinds of scenarios that are scary, embarrassing and horrific – all before that person opens the door or answers the phone.

The reason for this is because the human mind is amazingly powerful and has the ability to create concepts... concepts that have no basis in reality.

## Why Your Mind Can Work Against You

When presented with a situation either real or imagined, the mind will access all of its 'files' – which include all memories and life experiences – in order to determine how that person would usually deal with a particular situation. If the mind can't find a file because it has no previous experience on which to base a solution, it's capable of making one up. In other words, the human mind can take a situation that the person has never experienced before and create an entire script around it – even providing dialogue to all of the actors that it invents – to create an outcome!

Fascinating and scary, right?

Have you ever found yourself in a mild confrontation – maybe in line at the grocery store, in traffic or in a restaurant – and hours later come up with the 'perfect' response? That's a very simple example of the mind's ability to conceptualize scenarios and create outcomes.

Another example is the way many of us create resentments against people we've wronged or betrayed. Very often, the 'guilty' persons can't stand the destruction of their self-esteem in having to admit they are wrong. So they wriggle out of their shame by transferring it into resentments against the people who trigger the shame. We resent people because we have wronged them. A ridiculous injustice and, of all ridiculous injustices, one of the most universal.

At this point, perception truly is reality, for the human body cannot tell the difference between emotions resulting from a fabrication of the mind and an actual event.

### Figure 1 - How The Mind Works

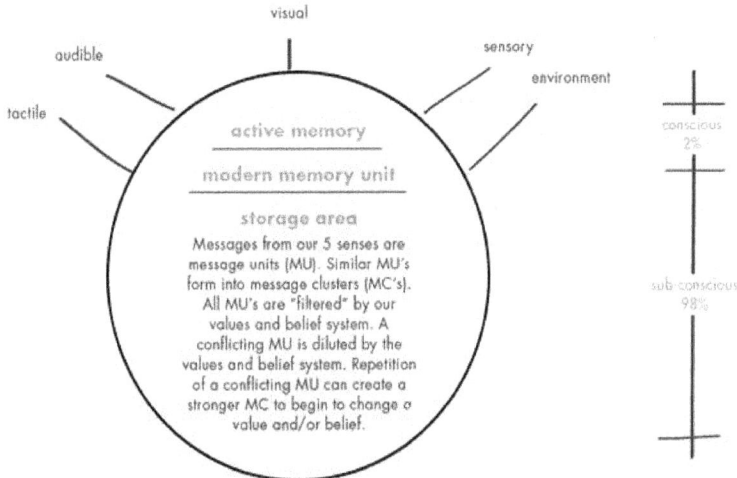

**Belief Systems**

Initially established by:

-culture

-religion

-authority figures


We change our belief systems through repetition --- change a habit practicing another habit until it is stronger. Experiential learning is stronger than theoretical.


**Purpose of the Mind**

-assess and evaluate

-decide (form judgments)

-instruct the brain

-storage of memory units


As shown in the previous illustration, Message Units (MUs) enter the Active/Conscious portion of the mind from all five sources. Research shows that

the Active/Conscious Mind can juggle five to nine activities at a time; this is why you can carry on a conversation and be thinking of other things at the same time. Depending on how busy it is, MUs 'download' from the Active/Conscious into the Modern Memory Unit approximately once every 1½ hours; then they're held in the Modern Memory Unit for 12 to 24 hours, at which time they are then downloaded into the long-term storage portion of the mind and filed as memories.

**Our Values and Beliefs systems are established by the following:**

*Culture*

In North America, people from different geographical regions, cities or towns have their own culture wherein they do certain things in a slightly different way. This cultural difference is not necessarily related to ethnicity. In larger cities, even different parts of the same city have differing cultures. For instance, New York City, Toronto, Montreal and Los Angeles each have many different cultures within their boundaries – some ethnic and others not.

A good example of a cultural value or belief is the fat/thin issue. In food-starved areas, only the wealthy can afford to be fat. In those places, being fat is a status symbol and in those cultures, fat people are seen to be more attractive than thin people. In areas where food is plentiful and only wealthy people can afford to both eat well and pay to get fit, fat is considered 'bad' and thin is 'in'.

## Religion

This doesn't only refer to people actively involved in formal religions. Atheists and agnostics may not believe in God but they usually have a belief that there's some kind of power greater than themselves – even if only in someone or something with a greater level of knowledge and/or training.

However, if someone undertakes religious training while they're very young, it's likely that that person will have a very well-honed sense of guilt. Picture an eight-year-old child being educated about mortal and venial sins by a well-meaning religion teacher. The teacher tells the child that some sins will be forgiven but certain others will result in the death of the soul, and yet others will result in the sinner burning in Hell for 300 years. To an eight-year-old, 300 years is a very long time! This is because children are literal. They feel terrible guilt and shame if they go on to commit many of those sins, simply because they have offended their own Values and Beliefs system.

## *Authority Figures*

This is the biggie. We use authority figures as models for certain behaviors, attitudes or beliefs, or we use them as an example of something we really don't want to be. Either way, they influence us. During our first 10 or 12 years when we're building our personalities, we typically spend more time with people who aren't our parents or family members. This is when we adopt some Values and Beliefs contrary to what our parents might like. This explains why every parent at one time or another has asked their child, "Where did you learn that?"

For instance, on the first day of school we might see a bully in the schoolyard and be very intimidated by them. We evaluate the situation and reach one of three possible conclusions:

- We really dislike the bullying behavior and determine we'll never be like that;
- Although we're afraid of the bully, we perceive that this is an excellent way to manage others, so we become a bully, or;
- We become anti-bullying crusaders, maybe even going so far as to bully the bullies with political correctness!

A strong authority figure makes us believe that we 'can' or we 'can't'. If an authority figure encourages our curiosity, takes time to show us how to do things, and tells us that being attractive to others is an attitude and not a particular image of physical beauty or style of dress, then we'll see the world differently than someone who had an authority figure who convinced them that they were stupid, worthless or ugly.

Tell someone long enough and often enough, or at the wrong moment in time, that they are stupid, worthless or ugly, and they will believe it – and worse, become it.

If you think kids aren't that easily influenced, consider how easy it is to convince them that there are monsters under the bed, or ghosts, goblins, or that Santa Claus is a real live person in the North Pole. These concepts become real because young kids are literal, and they believe what their authority figures tell them – especially if they love or fear their authority figure. The same authority figure can be forgiving, kind, and loving, or one who will punish and should be feared.

### *Right Or Wrong/Good Or Bad*

It's very difficult to evaluate our relationships from a position of right and wrong or good and bad, because it presumes that we all have the same Values and Beliefs systems. And in physical confrontations, the stronger side is always right! As Napoleon said, "God is on the side of the big battalions," – which relates to two armies battling one another when each 'knows' that they are chosen or favored by God (or Buddha, or Mohammed, or whoever).

In a religious context, suppose that one person is Roman Catholic and they have been well-schooled in their religion. Suppose further that the Roman Catholic person has a good friend who is a Muslim and also well-schooled in their own religion. To solve the problem of religious intolerance, and in the interest of world peace, imagine what would happen if the Roman Catholic and the Muslim locked themselves in a room and committed to not coming out until they decided who was right and who was wrong.

It is entirely possible that neither of them would ever see the light of day again.

Good or bad also poses problems. Imagine if one person was raised in an environment where dogs weren't household pets, but were considered working animals. They wouldn't likely feel an emotional connection to dogs and, when a dog's usefulness diminished, the dog would likely be destroyed and replaced with another working dog.

A person who kept dogs as household pets would be horrified by those actions. A debate over right and wrong would be useless, since the two people had an entirely different perspective of the issue because their Values and Beliefs were different. Similarly, if one person in a marriage was raised to believe in corporal punishment as a good parenting model, and the other person was raised to believe in the 'hugs and kisses' approach, they would never agree on who was right and who was wrong. Not a good thing for a marriage.

## *Knowing Vs. Believing*

Many people use the words 'know' when they mean 'believe' and they use 'knowledge' when they mean 'information'. One can believe in something without knowing it.

If we were to read or view an online video about building a watch, we might believe we could build a watch, but the only way we'll know how to build one is once we've done it.

Watching the video online is gathering information. Building the watch is gaining knowledge.

## *Open-mindedness*

Those of us who truly have an open mind see nothing strange in broken 'rules' – other than an opportunity to probe a little deeper into the inexplicable universe. These are people who 'believe' anything is possible, given the right set of circumstances. Truly open-minded people are those who can suspend their core beliefs for a time in order to investigate other options or approaches.

Ignorance is defined as 'a lack of knowledge' and is different from being stupid. An ignorant person might not have had much opportunity to learn, or may be tied to their core beliefs, such as racists who hate people whom they may never have met, or hate an entire race based on extremely limited contact. Their opinion is usually given to them by someone who is an authority figure. Ignorant people engage in judgment without benefit of knowledge.

Because Message Units form into clusters, which are stronger than a single Message Unit, it means that we believe things more strongly when we hear them repeated. Conversely, in order to overcome a cluster or a Values and Beliefs system that is causing us harm, we have to strengthen another Message Unit through repetition until it forms a cluster stronger than the old (unwanted) cluster or our old Values and Beliefs system.

For instance, if a person is told over and over and over for most of their formative, impressionable years that they're no good, they're stupid and will never amount to anything – chances are at age 30, 40 or 50, those messages will come true. People who believe they are no good, stupid and will never amount to anything continuously sabotage anything of value because they don't believe they are capable of anything else.

Can we change the way we think? The answer is yes!

We can change the way we think by reprogramming the 'messaging', isolating the reality of the situation and getting rid of all of the garbage fantasy projection.

How do we do that?

**By writing it down**. Seeing our thoughts on paper makes them real and also acts as a way to filter out what isn't or wasn't real.

Once the reality is uncovered, it needs to be acknowledged until it becomes the strong, dominant message.

Write down what you want to become based in reality. Repetition (practice) allows us to become what we are capable of becoming.

For example, if a battered spouse did this exercise, it could look like this:

> *"My name is Mary and I've been married to Clark for 14 years. Clark started calling me ugly names and being violent when we were dating. I thought that it would get better if we got married. It didn't. I am tired of being abused. I deserve to be treated better. I am*

*worthy of a noble love. I want to be strong, independent and to financially support myself. I want to divorce Clark. I am strong enough and smart enough. I can do this. I will have a fabulous life."*

What would your reprogramming look like? Write it down here:

_____
_____
_____
_____
_____
_____
_____
_____
_____
_____
_____
_____
_____
_____
_____
_____
_____

## THE HUMAN MIND

The human mind has two distinct parts: the Conscious and Subconscious.

*Figure 2 - The Conscious And Subconscious Mind*

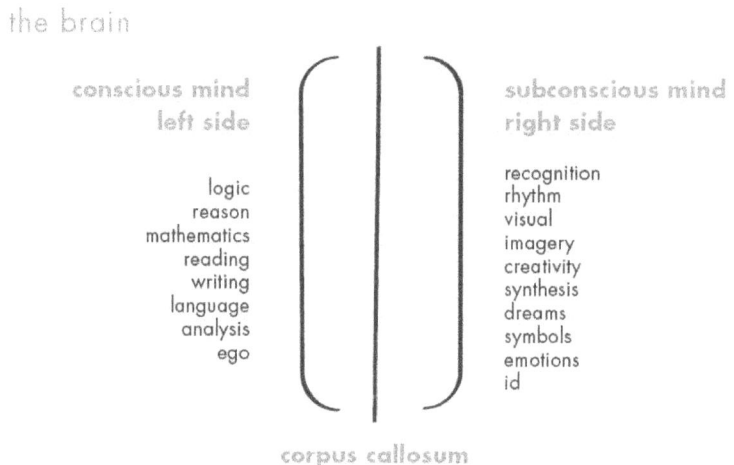

The left side contains our Conscious Mind, which helps with our daily decision-making and works according to the reality principle. It is intelligent, realistic, logical and proactive – especially in new situations where we have to apply rational thought processes to work out what to do and how to do it. All of our rational, logical planning and thinking goes on here. Our Conscious Mind works slowly, is only capable of managing seven things (± 2) at any one time, and is prone to overloading.

The right side of our brain houses our Subconscious Mind, which works 24 hours a day on 'auto pilot', reacting very quickly to physical, emotional, real, imagined or remembered events. It avoids pain, seeks to obtain pleasure, and survive without external considerations and without being rational or appropriate.

Our Subconscious Mind governs our emotions, imagination, memories and autonomic nervous system, which controls the function of our internal organs. These four main functions are very closely interlinked and mean that the mind affects the body and the body affects the mind.

Let that sink in …

The mind affects the body, and the body affects the mind.

## CONTROL CAR THEORY

*Figure 3 - A Balanced Example*

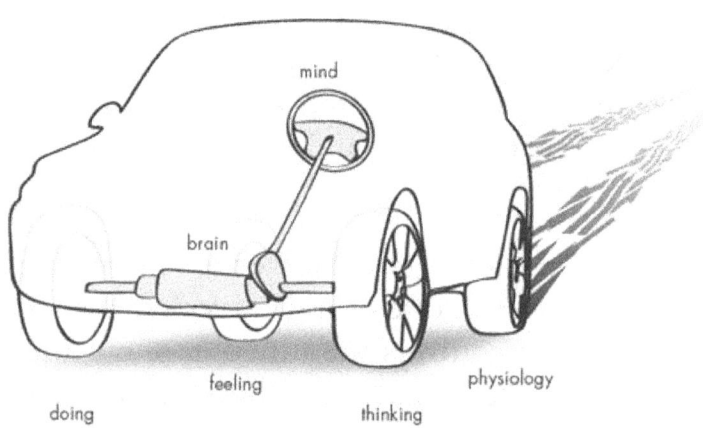

The human body is a smart system that's never been fully duplicated in nature. No other living thing has the power of thought and implementation that a human has, nor the ability for change or correction. A front-wheel drive car, like the one pictured above, with well-balanced 'tires', will drive us properly in the direction we want to go. First, there's a thought – which is followed by feelings, actions and physiological response.

Any major elevation in one or more of our behaviors would have the same effect as greatly overinflating a particular tire. Similarly, repression of our behaviors has the same effect as deflating a particular tire. Either way, it'll cause us to feel 'unbalanced'.

### Figure 4 - An Unbalanced Example

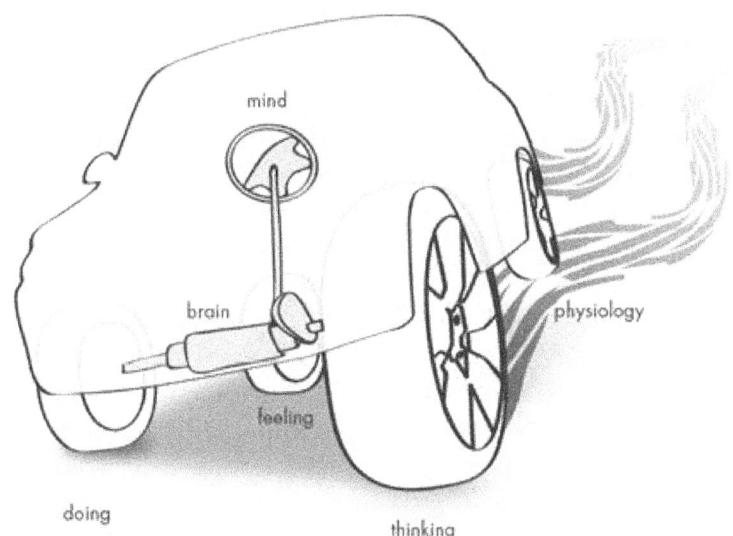

In the example shown opposite, the thinking 'tire' is obsessive (greatly inflated), the feelings are 'somewhat' inflated, and the actions are 'somewhat' deflated (becomes less active). Do it long enough and your health (physiology) could suffer. This car would not steer well – it would not be taking you in the direction you want to go.

## CONTROL COMPUTER THEORY

The Control Computer Theory illustrates how we can change our thinking to change our life.

Computer manufacturers mimic the way the human mind works by using us as the model for their products. The human mind is very smart, and the way computers query and sort information somewhat mirrors the human ability for change and correction. The way to change how we think is by trying out a new 'program'.

Since all change is stressful, it is comforting to know that the old program will always be in our memory (or hard drive), allowing us the choice between old and new behaviors (or programs). If at any time we want to revisit our old behaviors, we just have to access our memory and take a look. In addition, if the new behaviors are too extreme, we can replace them with another new program – totally new or a blend of our old behavior and the new.

A keyboard represents our thoughts and the monitor represents our mind, which forms judgments. A computer's 'judgments' are saved in the memory of one or more drives, while ours are saved in our mind's memory. By hitting 'Print', the computer performs an action attached to the thought.

If you key information into a computer program that isn't compatible, your computer will either produce garbage (bizarre behaviors) or it will reject it (contrary belief systems). To process it properly, the computer will need a new program.

The subconscious part of your mind is the storage area, which holds all of the information that you've accumulated throughout your lifetime; every experience, everything you've seen, heard, felt, smelled, touched and experienced. And it's all filed away as Message Units sorted into message clusters, or topics.

If you were a computer, your Subconscious Mind would be the hard drive. Your Conscious Mind would be the RAM (random access memory), and your Values and Beliefs systems would be the program.

## *Figure 5 - Control Computer*

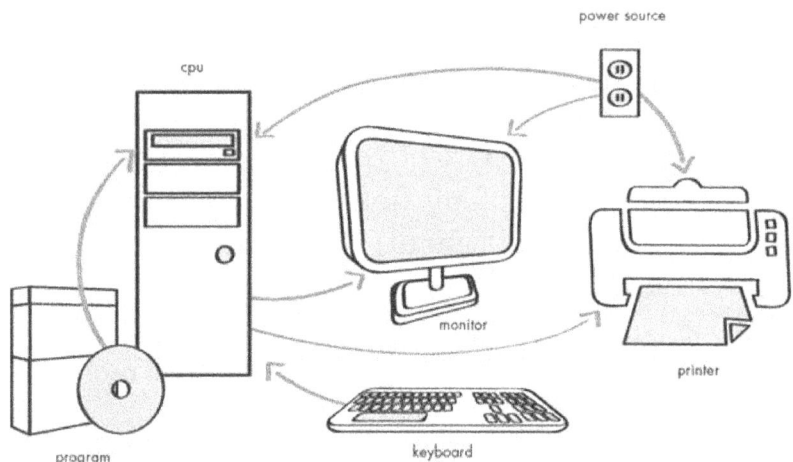

The major difference between the human mind and a computer is that the human mind has the ability to create concepts, whereas a computer can only deal with information that it has.

Let that sink in ...

If we think about a problem that has no readily available answer because we haven't experienced it before, our human mind will come up with outlandish and crazy search results that we have no business paying attention to.

A computer can be programmed to make projections, but it does not spontaneously create concepts. To your mind, perception is reality. In many instances, if your mind can conceive it, your body will follow.

The function of the Conscious Mind is to take in information, and the Subconscious Mind takes responsibility for filing and retrieving that information, and for weighing information against your Values and Beliefs systems. The new information is strengthened or diluted depending upon whether it matches our Values and Beliefs systems.

The Subconscious Mind exists to serve us and will try to find a way for us to get what we want, sometimes to our own detriment. For example:

A person sits on the edge of his bed, ready for sleep, and thinks, "Well, I suppose I'll toss and turn all night, and not get any sleep." Their subconscious will do everything it can to oblige them by interrupting their sleep.

Or, prior to going to sleep, that person considers some unpleasant things they're scheduled to do the next day. They think, "Man, tomorrow will probably be a really terrible day." Their subconscious will do everything it can to oblige them by putting them in a sour mood.

A computer, when asked to find information that it doesn't have, will search its files and then provide a message advising that the information was not found, then ask whether you want it to continue searching. We must then select one of two options – continue searching or cancel.

The human mind, on the other hand, when asked to find information that it does not have, will search and search and search to no end. It does not provide a message asking whether you want it to continue or cancel, and its ability to create concepts can provide some very interesting results. For example:

A person is seriously troubled by a financial problem, and has no training or experience in solving this type of problem. Their mind will search for solutions that do not exist. They're obsessed, because this problem really offends their Values and Beliefs, so they think and think and think. At some point, they may ask themselves, "What's going to happen if I can't solve this serious financial problem?" Their mind might take this as an instruction to create a concept, and the concept may create a picture of the person ending up living on the street and eating out of garbage bins – their life ruined; a disgrace. If that's not bad enough, their body will react to that concept – or perception – as though it was real.

Imagine a person has been threatened with extreme physical violence by someone they're afraid of. They have no experience in dealing with a situation like this. They think and think about what to do, and no answer appears. Their mind creates a concept

whereby every noise in the house represents someone breaking in, and they see an intruder in every shadow. At some point, the stress will drive them into total collapse – even if the threat was never, ever, actually carried out.

Here's another example: a person who is afraid of the dark is locked in a room with no light source. Within a period of time, they will begin to imagine terrifying presences. Although in reality nothing is there, their body reacts as though the concept is real.

Let that sink in …

To the human mind, perception is reality. In many instances, if a mind can conceive it that mind and body can achieve it – regardless if the concept is helpful or hurtful.

## OUR BASIC HUMAN NEEDS

In psychology, it's assumed that people have certain basic needs. These needs have been broken down in similar ways by four so-called experts and an overview of their findings is below:

In 1943, Professor Abraham Maslow described the 'Hierarchy of Needs':

> Self-actualization
>
> Esteem
>
> Love/belonging
>
> Safety
>
> Physiology

His theory states that one must satisfy lower-level basic needs before progressing on to meet higher-level growth needs. Once the lower level needs have been reasonably satisfied, one may be able to reach the highest level, called self-actualization.

> *"Every person is capable and has the desire to move up the hierarchy toward a level of self-actualization. Unfortunately, progress is often disrupted by failure to meet lower level needs. Life experiences, including divorce and loss of*

*job, may cause an individual to fluctuate between levels of the hierarchy." - Maslow*

Maslow noted only one in a hundred people become fully self-actualized because our society rewards motivation primarily based on esteem, love and other social needs. He was quoted as saying, "The story of the human race is the story of men and women selling themselves short."

In 1991, Manfred Max-Neef, assisted by Antonio Elizalde and Martin Hopenhayn, classified nine human needs as fundamental and universal:

Subsistence

Protection

Affection

Understanding

Participation

Leisure

Creation

Identity

Freedom

According to Max Neef, needs are also defined according to the existential categories of being, having, doing and interacting.

> *"We have reached a point in our evolution in which we know a lot. We know a hell of a lot. But we understand very little. Never in human history has there been such an accumulation of knowledge like in the last 100 years. Look how we are. What was that knowledge for? What did we do with it? And the point is that knowledge alone is not enough, that we lack understanding."* - Max Neef

In 1965, Dr. William Glasser hypothesized the theory that all people are born with specific basic needs that, if left unmet, lead to disharmony or disturbance. He described those basic human needs as follows:

> Power - A sense of winning or achieving, or a sense of self-worth
>
> Love and Belonging - To a family, to a community, or to other loved ones
>
> Freedom - To be independent, maintain your own personal space, autonomy
>
> Fun - To achieve satisfaction, enjoyment, and a sense of pleasure

Survival - Basic needs of shelter, survival, food, sexual fulfillment

Unlike some new therapies, Dr. Glasser's approach was emphatically drug-free and built on traditions of self-reliance. His attitude was that patients had to be worked with as if they have choices to make by demanding "What are you going to do about your life, beginning today?"

Glasser was quoted as saying, *"If everyone could learn that what is right for me does not make it right for anyone else, the world would be a much happier place."*

In 1991, Anthony (Tony) Robbins wrote about six human needs and described them as follows:

Certainty - assurance you can avoid pain and gain pleasure

Uncertainty/Variety - the need for the unknown, change, new stimuli

Significance - feeling unique, important, special or needed

Connection/Love - a strong feeling of closeness or union with someone or something

Growth - an expansion of capacity, capability or understanding

> Contribution - a sense of service and focus on helping, giving to and supporting others

Robbins believes everyone is – and can be – motivated by their desire to fulfill these needs and he urges us to consider these needs when thinking about developing and delivering products and services to people. According to Robbins, the question to ask is, *"What need or needs does my product fulfill for my customer?"*

> *"Beliefs have the power to create and the power to destroy. Human beings have the awesome ability to take any experience of their lives and create a meaning that disempowers them or one that can literally save their lives."*
> - Anthony Robbins

In Dynamic Discovery, we classify the basic human needs under five headings:

> Love and Belonging - includes sex, families or loved ones, as well as groups

> Achievement, Power and Recognition - includes feeling worthwhile as well as winning

> Freedom - includes independence, autonomy, and your own 'space'

> Fun - includes pleasure and enjoyment

> Survival - includes nourishment and shelter

We apply the acronym **LAFFS** to make the five needs easier to remember.

Whether we're aware of it or not, we're always acting to meet these needs – but we don't necessarily act effectively. Socializing with people is an effective way to meet our need for belonging, while isolating and self-pitying in the hope that people will come to us is generally an ineffective way of meeting that need. As a matter of fact, it can be painful and costly (in psychological terms).

If life is unsatisfactory, if we're distressed or in trouble, a quick check of whether we're meeting our four basic LAFF needs (the fifth, Survival, is implied) because it's often in an attempt to meet those needs that we run into trouble.

## KNOWING WHAT WE WANT

We don't typically think of meeting our Love and Belonging need when we wonder whether a friend would be able to meet us for lunch or plan a group event. We may want to meet a friend, we may want to mingle with a group or want 'our' football team or 'our' political party to win.

What usually drives us as social beings is our wants, since we don't think of our needs as something we require. We think of what we want, behave to get what we want, fantasize about what we want and so on. We can check whether we are meeting our wants through addressing three basic questions:

> What is it I want?

> What am I doing to get what I want?

> Is it working?

In order to get what we want, we need to make a plan that's workable and something we can successfully implement. In other words, it concentrates on things that are within our control.

A person might not be able to make their spouse talk to them, but they can talk to their spouse.

A person may not be able to make their teenage son treat them with respect, but they can decide that they will no longer provide a laundry and catering service to a son who treats them with contempt.

A person may not be able to make the company they work for give them a promotion, but they can look for a promotion, lobby for it, and apply for the job when it comes up.

In this way, we are empowered by focusing on the power of doing what is within our control.

**Doing**

Emotions are a wonderful, immediate and 'alive' source of information about how we're doing and whether we're happy with what's going on in our lives. But it is very, very hard to change our emotions directly.

It is easier to change our thinking – to decide, for example, that we'll no longer think of ourselves as victims, that we'll concentrate on thinking about what we can do rather than what everybody else ought to do.

Changing what we do is the key to changing how we feel and to getting what we want.

Sometimes we find ourselves so caught up in anger, depression or resentment that even changing how we think seems an impossible task. In such situations, a positive change in what we do may be the best we can manage.

**Control**

Control plays a part in meeting our needs, and we all control in different ways. Whereas one person seeks control through position and money, another wants to control their physical space (like the teenager who bans all parents and parent-like persons from their room). Similarly, one wants to chair the committee, another wants an office with a corner and two windows, and yet another wants a specific meal on the table at precisely 6:30 p.m.

Control gets us into trouble in two distinct ways: when we try to control other people, and when we use drugs and alcohol to give us a false sense of control. At the very heart is the idea that 'The only person I can really control is myself'.

If we think we can control others, or if we think others can control us, we move in the direction of frustration.

There are things that 'happen' to all of us that we aren't personally responsible for, but we can choose what we do about these things. Trying to control other people is a losing game – a never-ending battle that alienates us from others and causes endless pain and frustration.

This is why it is vital to stick to what is within our own control, and to respect the right of other people to meet their needs. We can get a false sense of control from alcohol and some other drugs. Unfortunately, our lives are never more out of control than when we are drunk or drugged. There are very few people in this world who ever woke up with a hangover to find that they had fewer problems than they had the night before.

This goes for any obsessive behavior. Those obsessions need to be replaced by doing something else, and that something else – whatever it is – has to have a fair chance of getting us what we want in life. Many people working in the addiction and behavior modification fields have found this approach useful.

## Using The Past To Create Change

Counseling is often thought to involve delving into the past and, in many cases, it is – but in Dynamic Discovery, we probably visit the past to a lesser extent than those who use other approaches to behavior change. This is not a criticism of other approaches, but shows how Dynamic Discovery is different.

In Dynamic Discovery, the past is merely seen as the source of our wants and of our ways of behaving.

Not only are the bad things that happened to us in our past, but our successes are there, too. Our focus is to learn what needs to be learned about the past, and then move on to empowering us to satisfy our needs and wants now and in the future through the knowledge that it is our perceptions that influence our behaviors.

We are products of the past, but we do not have to go on being its victims.

# PART 2

Whether you're reading this book as an individual or as part of a group workshop, after reading Part 1 of Dynamic Discovery, you should have a basic understanding of why your mind works the way it does, why it's failed you in the past and why you'll succeed in the future.

Part 2 of Dynamic Discovery will give you specific examples of how others navigated the program and the answers they found for themselves.

One of the most important elements of Dynamic Discovery is the emphasis on the 'solution'. No module or session should end on a sour note. Instead, each person should end each chapter focused on the positive. Because the only way to convince people to commit to and participate in the Dynamic Discovery process is to give them what they want. So that's precisely what we'll do.

So we're going to ask "What do you want?" and then focus on "How can you get it?" In short, we end each module's work with the solution, not the problem.

The technique of paying attention to our individual wants and needs in a positive, non-critical head space is what will set the Dynamic Discovery process apart from other traditional methods.

Each and every person who participates in Dynamic Discovery is guaranteed a safe environment, free from criticism or judgment based on some previous behavior – a setting where we can feel free to evaluate our own lives based on how it is our lives are working, and not based on the concepts of 'good or bad' or 'right or wrong'. Participants – whether in person in a group setting or as an individual participant – will not be attacked for their thinking. Instead, all participants will be given a chance to change their beliefs about themselves. This is all based upon personal self-evaluation, where we find the outcome and effects on our lives are immense and far-ranging.

In Dynamic Discovery, the people we work with are usually not only experts at punishment, but also experts at believing and/or knowing how they have been punished by others. Does this apply to you? Frequently, self-punishers seek help because of the lengths to which they have gone to punish themselves. The 'turning point' is often the moment when we grasp the concept of consequence. It is important that a consequence should be used to improve our lives as opposed to punishing ourselves – in other words, to constructively use consequences to stop negative behavior without undoing any progress that we might have already made. More effective results will be obtained once we are able to determine and give ourselves permission to choose our own fates.

Dynamic Discovery consistently focuses on you, the individual, and your own personal crisis. We acknowledge the challenge but turn our attention away from the very issues that may have produced the problem and we focus instead on finding a solution. We learn to consider behavior outcomes as very real things.

The benefit of Dynamic Discovery is that you'll be able to come up with behaviors that are just as real as your old ones, but without the same painful outcomes. The new behaviors will help you get what you want.

Do you feel alone in your pain, with no one to recognize your need or desire to change? You're not alone. As a matter of fact, most people in these circumstances find it unimaginable that anyone else is struggling with change. Dynamic Discovery is where you'll learn that many people are seeking change, as well as a desire to simply live happy, peaceful lives.

## CONTROL THEORY

All humans are motivated by basic needs. They are the need for:

**Love and Belonging**

**Achievement, Power and Recognition**

**Freedom**

**Fun**

**Survival**

Again, we use the acronym **LAFFS** as a reminder of the five basic needs; and our motivation to satisfy these needs is very powerful. Everything we think, feel and do is in response to one of those five basic needs.

> We call a friend for a chat and our need for **Love and Belonging** is met.

> We strive to get an award at work and our **Achievement, Power and Recognition** need is met.

> We open our own business so we can be our own boss, and our need for **Freedom** is met.

> We play tennis and our need of **Fun** is met.

We eat breakfast and our need to **Survive** is met.

Sometimes one action can meet more than one need, but the basic premise is the same.

But often what we do to satisfy our needs isn't as blatantly obvious as the examples given above. Behavior is not always blatantly obvious to the observer. 'Total Behavior' includes doing, thinking, feeling and physiology as components.

When we once again compare a person to a front-wheel-drive car, the front wheels consist of thinking and doing – the two most easily manipulated behaviors – and the rear wheels are feeling and physiology. In order to change the direction the back wheels travel, we need to first change the direction of the front wheels.

We've all heard someone refer to a situation where they believed their reaction to be inappropriate: "I just didn't know what to do, so I didn't do anything."

Although they didn't take any outward action, the statement "I didn't do anything" is completely false. The thinking behavior was undoubtedly going full speed, with thoughts and ideas surfacing and being tossed out in rapid succession. The feeling behavior was likely feeling panicked and helpless. The physiology behavior may have been choosing rapid breathing and palm sweating. Although the 'doing

behavior' itself may have appeared to have been frozen, it was actively keeping the person still, and could very well be the reason the person is around to tell the tale.

In order to better explain the Control Theory concept, below is a list of behaviors that you might employ when 'getting your needs met' has been threatened. They could include:

## DYNAMIC DISCOVERY BOOK

### *Table 1 - Behavior Examples*

| | | | |
|---|---|---|---|
| Dominating | Abusing | Accepting | Envying |
| Angering | Being Anxious | Fearing | Arguing |
| Avoiding | Gambling | Blaming | Bullying |
| Gossiping | Cheating | Complaining | Controlling |
| Creating | Criticizing | Crying | Deceiving |
| Depressing | Discriminating | Being Dishonest | Drugging |
| Listening | Intruding | Lusting | Becoming |
| Rejecting | Lying | Punishing | Resenting |
| Shouting | Smoking | Spying | Thieving |
| Swearing | Threatening | Understanding | Victimizing |

It's important to note that when our needs are threatened, we'll always respond with a behavior. The fact that people view the same circumstance in a different light is understandable since these needs and threats to needs, although universal, are very personal. The thinking behavior is only one component of the Total Behavior system and the combination of components is greater than just the thinking component alone. If, at any level, the entire system perceives a need as being unmet, the whole system will respond. The question is not whether we are or aren't behaving, but whether the behaviors we are using are helping us get what we really want, i.e. happiness, peace, etc.

Now, let's create a 'want' list that directly relates to our LAFFS needs, where each item we list can be connected to an underlying need. When composing a list of what you want, it should define your individual idea of your Ideal World. What might constitute a picture of ultimate happiness for one might appear to be a mediocre existence for another. Our own idea of an Ideal World is very personalized and, therefore, one person's idea of 'ideal' might be in direct conflict with the 'ideal' of someone close to them.

Our Ideal World is a "personal picture album" of all the people, things, ideas, and ideals that increase the quality of our lives. Our Ideal World is a personal thing. Satisfaction isn't determined by the specific pictures, but by how well you see your reality matching your pictures.

While the Basic Human Needs are the general motivation for all human behavior, the Ideal World is the specific motivation. The Basic Human Needs describe what we need; the Ideal World pictures detail how we meet them. The Basic Human Needs are universal; our Ideal Worlds are unique.

The pictures in our Ideal World:

    Meet one or more of our Basic Human Needs

Are changing and changeable

Are unique

Often conflict with each other

Vary in levels of intensity

Vary in levels of attainability

To gain a clearer understanding of your personal Ideal World, consider the following:

Who are the most important people in your life?

What are your most deeply held values?

If you became the person you would ideally like to be, what traits or characteristics would you have?

What is an accomplishment that you are really proud of?

If you could have the perfect job, what would that be?

If you were independently wealthy, what would you do with your time?

Describe a time in your life you would call a peak experience.

What does it mean to be a friend?

What brings a significant amount of meaning to your life?

What, for you, makes a house a home?

What have you learned about your Ideal World?

What have you learned about your Ideal World pictures in general?

Now think about the following...

If your Ideal World picture is of your son, "the athlete," you may be unhappy if he turns out to be a scholar, while a parent with a scholarly picture would be thrilled with a studious son. A parent with a picture of a loving, devoted son might see athletic or scholarly accomplishment as equally irrelevant.

Similarly, if your Ideal World picture of a spouse is that of a poet laden with flowers and wine, then you won't feel satisfied if the spouse of your reality arrives with chicken wings, beer, and the TV Guide!

There are also pictures of yourself in your Ideal World – that is, the self that you want to see. You might have pictures of your appearance, your personality, your weight. Cosmetic companies, plastic surgeons, and diet organizations improve the reality of their bottom lines by promising to reduce

the gap between how you are and how you want to see yourself.

How can knowing your Ideal World be helpful to you?

It's within your power to be more satisfied and to reduce the gap between your reality and your Ideal World. There are two approaches you can use: you can change your reality to bring it closer to your Ideal World, or you can change the pictures in your Ideal World.

If the gap between reality and your Ideal World picture concerns something that you can control, you can use that gap as a motivator to change your reality. For example, owning a home is an Ideal World picture for many people. Knowing that, you can use strategies to make it reality: create a plan, save your money, shop strategically, and so on. The clearer your picture, the more likely you are to recognize it when it's in front of you.

However, many Ideal World pictures are neither tangible nor controllable. We might have pictures of how other people should behave, or even of how the weather should be. For example, how did the reality of last winter match your Ideal World?

Sometimes, the best way to reduce the gap is to change your picture. If you don't like winter and you can't change your reality (i.e. move away), then consider changing your picture of winter. Embrace the good fortune of living in a climate of changing seasons!

Okay, maybe that's too much to ask. However, realize that it'll be difficult to feel happy and satisfied if your Ideal World is filled with rigid pictures of things over which you have no control, such as pictures of what other people should be doing. Others seldom do what we think they should! And while you may have influence, do you have any control over their behavior, really?

Remember: some things are important; others are not. Some things are under our control; others are not. When something is important but not under our control, examining and changing our Ideal World picture may be helpful.

Sometimes, changing our Ideal World picture is the only way to reduce the gap. For example, when a loved one passes away, we are faced with a reality totally out of our control. Does that mean that this person is now removed from our Ideal World? Not at all. We can change our pictures away from shared activities in present or future to pictures of the meaning that person has brought to our lives, or to how we might now live while honoring them.

The important things that we do are attempts to satisfy pictures in our Ideal World. If you'd like to give this a try, pick one small area in your life where you feel dissatisfied. Compare your reality with your Ideal World picture. Then, examine whether it's better to change your reality or to change your Ideal World picture. See what happens!

For example, this is how a conversation using the Dynamic Discover process would go if a client (in this case, a husband) believed his wife should 'change her attitude'?

| | |
|---|---|
| *DD:* | *What would it mean to you if your wife changed her attitude?* |
| *Client:* | *Then I would be happy.* |
| *DD:* | *If you could be happy and your wife wouldn't have to change, how would that be?* |
| *Client:* | *Okay, I guess.* |
| *DD:* | *Which do you really want – your wife to change or you to be happy?* |
| *Client:* | *I want to be happy.* |
| *DD:* | *Being happy is more important?* |
| *Client:* | *Yes, being happy is more important.* |

In this situation (and many, many others), our Dynamic Discovery participant thought the only way he could achieve happiness was if his partner changed her behavior. The thing is – happiness is never found in an external source. It's found in you, and never in the changes that any other person could make. At best, another person can only enhance your life. If you believe that your life is dependent on the actions of another, then you are ceding entire control over your thoughts, feelings, and actions to that other person – and if that person was to leave or die, you would be left in a psychological wasteland; a type of human purgatory.

It's a good idea to explore what being happy would look like to you when you get what you want, and we will explore how to do just that later on in this book.

The whole point of Dynamic Discovery is to reveal the concept of Total Behavior and to help you develop a habit of looking at yourself in terms of all the different behavioral components as you self-evaluate.

What you've done in the past isn't as important as how you perceive your past experiences and how they've impacted your life. This process isn't based on examining past behaviors, but on examining the effectiveness of these behaviors.

For example, with Dynamic Discovery, a person wanting to cope, manage or deal with an addiction or an obsession rather than focusing on the addiction or obsession will instead evaluate whether their past behaviors have obtained their desired effect. Moral or religious judgments have no place in this process since we are dealing with outcomes of behaviors, rather than the 'right' or 'wrong' of any action.

## INTRODUCTIONS

In an actual Dynamic Discovery group session, this conversation took place. The participant was a married man with two children who was restless and unhappy and claims to have never been in counseling or therapy:

> DD: *What's been going on in your life that caused you to come to this group?*
>
> Client: *I've pretty well gotten everything I ever wanted, and I know I should be content, but I'm not. I'm just not content.*
>
> DD: *What do you mean when you say you're not content?*
>
> Client: *I married a great woman, have a boy and a girl. I'm self-employed, I go to church and I get along with most other people, but... I'm just sort of unhappy.*
>
> DD: *What do you mean when you say you're unhappy?*
>
> Client: *I'm not excited about anything. I'm not motivated to do anything. Maybe I'm just depressed.*

DD: Are there one or two words to describe your circumstances?

Client: I don't know. Like what?

DD: Well, would you say feeling like that is confusing?

Client: Yes. Very confusing.

DD: You've done the things you thought would make you happy and now you find that it's not enough. So what have you done to try and resolve your feelings?

Client: A couple things.

DD: Like what?

Client: I tried to kick some of my bad habits. I swear less. I started taking more days off from the job. I tried talking to my wife. I even had an affair.

Note: We ignore the reference to having an affair as going over that behavior would be entertaining but not productive.

DD: What do you mean by 'bad habits'?

| | |
|---|---|
| Client: | Smoking, swearing and drinking with the boys. |
| DD: | Did you get drunk when you went out with the boys? |
| Client: | No. |
| DD: | How did all these things you tried work out for you? |
| Client: | Not very well, obviously. |
| DD: | Did they help you get what you want? |
| Client: | No. |
| DD: | Tell me, what DO you want? |
| Client: | I just want to get on in life. I want to know what went wrong. |
| DD: | And what would 'getting on in life' look like to you? |
| Client: | Well, I've always wanted to learn to fly a plane. |
| DD: | What would that mean to you, to learn to fly a plane? |

*Client:* I'd feel like I'd done something new and different, like I'd accomplished something.

*DD:* Give me one word to describe what it would feel like if you had all that.

*Client:* I'd feel free.

*DD:* So if you felt like you had accomplished something and you felt free, what would that mean to you?

*Client:* Well... I guess I'd be happy.

*DD:* Is that what you really want – to be happy?

*Client:* Yes.

This client was a man who wanted to be happy, but in reality he wasn't doing anything positive to serve that feeling. Smoking, swearing and drinking did not work for him. His life itself was the problem and he wasn't happy with it. His perception of his life and self-evaluation of how he felt about it were important here.

It's important that every Dynamic Discovery participant, whether in a group setting or as an individual, does their own evaluating, and that

nobody tells anyone what's wrong with the participant's life.

What would your introduction look like? Would you like to find a way to get what you want out of this process?

Another introduction might look like this one:

Our client is 23 years old, a recovering drug addict and the single parent of one child. Her child's father is an addict and she believed herself to be 'co-dependent'. She left school in tenth grade and has never had a 'real job'. She complains that her mother (with whom she and her child live) is "always telling her what to do." She states that everything she has ever tried to do has ended up a failure.

> DD: *What actions have you taken to try to deal with your situation?*
>
> Client: *For the past three years, I've been attending a 12-step recovery program and haven't really gotten anywhere. I've also tried several other types of counseling. I just can't seem to get it. I tried going back to school, but that didn't work because my mom refused to watch my son and I couldn't find anyone else. I tried to find another place to live, but I just don't have*

> enough money for a decent place, so I've given up on that. I tried to get some money from my baby's father, but I never can find him and when I can find him, I usually get into more trouble. After a day or two, we start fighting and then he is gone again and I still don't have any support money.

DD: Have these actions you've taken helped you to improve your situation?

Client: No. Not a bit. I try and fail and feel even worse!

Note: Although it may sound redundant, we reflect a bit more about the evaluation she just made.

DD: Have you been able to think of or do anything that has worked for you?

Client: No, and I'm miserable.

DD: What is it that you really want?

Client: I just want to be happy.

DD: That is a relative term. What does 'happy' mean to you?

Client: *If I was happy, I would have a job and a new boyfriend – one who would understand me. I would have my own place to live and I would have my high school diploma.*

DD: *If you had all that, what would it mean?*

Client: *I would feel like I was more in control of my life.*

DD: *And if you had more control of your life, what would that mean to you?*

Client: *I think I would feel more at peace. And I would feel strong.*

DD: *If we could find a way for you to feel strong, how would that be?*

Client: *That'd be great!*

It might seem that this method of arriving at what you want ignores a lot of important information, but the goal of Dynamic Discovery is to find solutions to individual challenges instead of wasting time and energy delving into the past or wringing out confessions.

Both of the above-quoted participants have made attempts to change their lives, but those attempts have not been successful. Both stated they "wanted to be happy," but happiness for one meant freedom – like being able to fly a plane – and happiness to the other meant a whole list of things, but the bottom line was that she would feel at peace and feel strong.

We could all make a list of tangible wants, but when we describe the feeling or sensation we think we'll get from achieving these wants, very few of us will want anything more than happiness, peace, contentment or strength.

Other therapy models might bond participants based on mutual pain. In Dynamic Discovery, we take the much more positive approach of identifying common wants so that we can make a start at getting what you want and need, regardless of past behaviors.

# FEELINGS

Let's focus on feelings and how they affect our lives. What kinds of feelings have you been struggling with? If we were to compile a list of all of the feelings that trouble you or have troubled you in the past, what would that list look like?

***Table 2 - Troubling Feelings***

| Fear | Guilt | Anger | Resentment |
|---|---|---|---|
| Loneliness | Isolation | Failure | Hopeless |
| Stupidity | Weakness | Useless | Sadness |
| Angst | Hate | Slighted | Ugly |
| Depressed | Unwanted | Unhealthy | |

Maybe like this? Feel free to add to the list. Generally, we won't have much difficulty describing feelings that have caused us the most disruption and discomfort in our lives.

Now look at the list above and pick one specific, unwanted feeling. Which one speaks to you the loudest? The one you identify with most? The one that you've struggled with the hardest? Circle it.

It's no surprise that we seem to have an endless supply of ways to describe how badly we've felt in the past or are feeling right now. In group sessions, lists of more than thirty different negative feelings are the norm!

It's safe to say that our lives are very much affected by the feelings on the list above. But how much? Well, how many hours a day do we deal with the feelings on this list? If we think of time in terms of a 24-hour day, if we had to pay to feel the feelings on the list above, how many hours would we have to pay for?

It's not unusual for some people to say they spend 12 to 18 hours a day somehow involved with these unwanted feelings. Others say they experience these feelings, on and off, for five or six hours a day. Sometimes, it's only one or two hours. Often after thinking about this for a while, some people will revise their answers to include more hours. Regardless of whether you're paying for these feelings for one hour a day or for 18 hours a day, the question is, "Are you spending on pain more than you want to pay?"

Yes? It only makes sense.

What about your sleep habits? Many Dynamic Discovery clients have trouble sleeping at night, and it's because the feelings we listed above are keeping them awake. Does this pertain to you?

We're often overwhelmed when we start consciously considering the amount of hours we spend each day on our negative emotions. From hours in a day to days in a week, it's not unusual to find we spend eight days a week with our own negativity.

Most of us understand that the 'fight or flight' response occurs very quickly in the short term, but few of us have considered that it's possible to live with these reactions over the course of an entire lifetime.

Going back to our list of unwanted feelings, fear is defined as "a distressing emotion aroused by impending danger, evil or pain."

Fear is a simple response to a threat. In Control Theory terms, when our needs aren't being met, we experience fear. Is fear a feeling you want to feel more of? No? Well, do you want to be able to respond appropriately to a threat? Yes? Let's find out how...

Fear is the 'driving feeling behind all other unwanted feelings'. In other words, fear is the root of our anger, guilt, loneliness and so on. For instance, what if you walked into a Mom and Pop store and just blatantly stole something? You might feel guilt because of a fear of getting caught stealing.

Well, what if you meet someone whom you like and who obviously likes you? Have you ever thought that this person wouldn't like you once they got to know you? It's the same thing. You're feeling guilt because you fear getting caught being yourself.

What about the other feelings on our list? How does fear pertain to them?

Anger is a feeling that easily masks fear. An angry person rarely appears to be full of fear, but if we accept fear as a simple response to a threat, we can see the fear in an angry person. Many people who use anger as a continuous controlling behavior are simply trying to meet their needs.

Now go back to the list. Try to make a connection for each of our unwanted feelings and fear. Ask yourself this: "Which feeling on the list have I not felt?"

Almost everyone will respond that they've felt all of those feelings at one time or another in their lives.

Dynamic Discovery participants routinely represent a wide cross-section of our society, and often include co-dependents and/or addicts who can typically describe actual events related to their drinking, drugging, co-depending, over-eating, or other obsessions – and these events are usually the result of the client's attempt to resolve how they are feeling at the time. The question we should ask ourselves is:

"Are our feelings the biggest problem we have?" In other words, if we could somehow feel better, would things be alright?

This question is a crucial one. It sets the stage for future connections we'll need to make between our thinking and doing behaviors, and it starts us thinking in an evaluative manner. Many of us will respond that our feelings are the single biggest difficulty we have in our lives and all we need is to simply feel better.

The desire to 'feel better' is one that bonds us. It's almost universal and an ongoing wish shared by almost everyone.

So now that we've established what the unwanted feelings we have are and the amount of time we've been spending on them, the next step is to determine the amount of difficulty we've been having with our feelings, and evaluate how successful our coping mechanisms have worked up until now.

A very basic evaluative question is, "How has this been working out for you?"

For example, if a person is feeling stressed and anxious at the end of every workday, and they have a few drinks to unwind, which turns into lots of drinks and they start almost every morning with a

hangover, we could ask, "How has this been working out for you?"

What are the feelings you have that you don't want and what have you done to feel better? Follow that thought up with "How has that been working out for you?" What would your answer be?

If you could live your life the way you wanted and feel better, would that appeal to you? It IS possible. You have a choice in the matter – and as we continue through Dynamic Discovery, you'll learn how to do just that.

For example, the following conversation occurred in an actual Dynamic Discovery group session. Our client has spent her entire life feeling guilt, and she's gotten nowhere.

| | |
|---|---|
| DD: | *You have tried to stop feeling guilty, right?* |
| Client: | *Yes.* |
| DD: | *Instead of talking about how you don't want to feel, can we focus on how you DO want to feel?* |
| Client: | *Okay.* |
| DD: | *And how would you like to be feeling?* |

Client:   I'd like to feel peaceful.

DD:   What does peaceful look like to you? Describe yourself being peaceful.

Client:   It looks like I am calm, and worry-free about being alone and lonely.

So what do YOU want? Let's make another list. It might look like this. Again, please add any of the feelings you'd want to feel more of below.

### Table 3 - Feelings You'd Like To Feel More Of

| Peaceful | Happy | Serene | Confident |
| Assured | Assertive | Successful | Attractive |
| Calm | Content | Respected | Powerful |
| Complete | Strong | | |

Fill in the blanks. I want to feel _____ and to me, _____ looks like:

_____

_____

_____

_____

_____

_____

The great news is it's possible to start feeling this way if you want to. The choice is yours. All you have to do is decide. The road to happiness means identifying and reaching for the feelings you want to be experiencing.

Have you tried to get rid of these old feelings by identifying them?

Chances are the answer to that question is "Yes."

And how is it working out for you?

This illustrates just how broken most of our coping mechanisms are, and how they've failed us.

Progress! By now, we've accomplished a great deal by seeing the commonality of our feelings and by deciding whether we want to find a better way to deal with our problems and start feeling better. At the end of the next section, which involves thinking, you'll be able to formulate more involved solutions to your problems.

# THINKING

The goal now is to make the connection between thoughts and feelings and to be able to see the connection between the 'thinking' and the 'feeling' wheels on the Control Car.

It's important to understand that how we feel about something or someone is often the result of what we're thinking about that situation or person. In addition, we'll investigate ways we can change how we're thinking and in turn, change how we are feeling.

This session is often a turning point. As described in the previous chapter on feelings, most of us used to believe that our feelings were our life's biggest problem. We also believed that there was nothing we could do to feel better. But we learned that our biggest problem was merely identifying what didn't work.

In order to show the connection between the 'feeling' and 'thinking' behaviors, we use an exercise developed by Dr. Glasser. Follow the instructions below, close your eyes and pause for about 30 seconds after each task:

    1.    Think of the color red.

    2.    Think of the color blue.

3. Think of the color yellow.

4. Be sad.

5. Be happy.

6. Raise your right hand.

Now that you've completed this exercise, which of the instructions was easiest to follow?

Was it Number 6, because it required so little thought and feeling?

When you thought of the color red, was it because you visualized a rose, a fire truck, or a stop sign?

What made you sad or what made you happy? Was it because you visualized something happy or sad? Being with people you love or the funeral of a loved one? This is a very personalized moment. What makes us happy and sad is a very individualistic experience.

Without fail, the easiest portions of this exercise are always when you have a clear picture in your mind of an object or an event which personified the color or feeling you were seeking.

Up to this point, most of us will have spent our entire lifetimes believing that the root of all our difficulties has been how we have been feeling, NOT what we have been thinking. Over the years we've been tossing some kind of behavior at our feelings, hoping to feel better, but with no success.

The preceding exercise shows that thinking is attached to memories and illustrates that you are in control of those thoughts.

'Secret thinking' is the thoughts we have which are only known by us alone. Dynamic Discovery participants often have a lot of secret thinking going on that they don't want anyone to know about, and one of the most common secret thoughts we have is that we're going crazy.

On the surface, it appears to those around us that we're doing okay. Inside, however, our thoughts are often spinning in high gear, like a mental tornado – which we refer to as 'Spin Dryer Thinking'.

For example, a recent Dynamic Discovery participant shared that at a time when he was overtaken by turbulent Spin Dryer Thinking, he gave himself what he thought was an appropriate nickname. Among other things, he saw himself as stupid and a failure and thought of himself as a "F*cking dummy."

What are the names you call yourself?

When we're not getting what we want and need, and partly because of our criticism-oriented society, we tend to blame ourselves. Despite outward appearances, we all secretly demean ourselves with negative descriptors and nicknames.

Think back… was there ever a time in your life when you thought you were stupid? Or a failure? Useless?

Of course. We all have had those thoughts. 'Hidden rules' are the ones we all live by They are the 'shoulds' and 'shouldn'ts', the 'can't dos' or 'could have dones', the 'musts' and the 'must nots' – just to name a few.

It's not unusual to change our behavior only to have the change sabotaged by the thought that we somehow 'could have done' better and we're left with the idea that what we did wasn't good enough. In many instances, we create an entire thinking process built around that one belief or thought about ourselves – that whatever we do isn't good enough or that we should have done better.

If you constantly think "Nothing I do is good enough" or "I should have done better," are you surprised that you don't feel good about yourself?

Sometimes people are tempted to think that if we just 'think positive', everything will be alright. Dynamic Discovery participants are no exception, and a recent exchange went like this:

> DD: Have you tried thinking positively?

*Client:*     *Yes.*

*DD:*     *And how did that turn out for you?*

*Client:*     *Not worth a damn.*

*DD:*     *How would it work out if you tried it again?*

*Client:*     *Not worth a damn.*

*DD:*     *Would you be interested in changing your thinking in a way that would be meaningful to you?*

*Client:*     *Of course!*

The above exchange demonstrates why Dynamic Discovery isn't merely a course in positive thinking. New choices are open to us if we want effective and meaningful change in life. Furthermore, these changes could affect our thinking and feeling if that's what we want.

Let's return to our list of feelings that we'd like to have more of, which we listed in Table 3. Instead of thinking of ourselves as losers or failures, let's figure out what we'd prefer to be thinking.

If you having difficulty figuring out what you want to be thinking, perhaps the following dialogue will help develop a clearer picture:

DD: What do you want?

Client: To be happy.

DD: If you were happy, what would you be thinking?

Client: That I was okay.

DD: What would okay look like to you?

Client: I don't know.

DD: Would you like to find out what that picture of okay would look like?

Client: Yes.

DD: If you were happy, what would you be doing?

Client: I'd be getting along well with my wife and my children. And the people at work. I would be pleasant with everyone and everyone would be glad to be around me. I'd be paying more attention to my wife and doing special things with my kids.

| DD: | And what would you be thinking when you were doing all these various activities? |
| Client: | I'd be thinking, "You are really a good person. You're fun. You're pleasant. People want to be around you. This is great. You are really a special guy." |

Because sometimes we have a hard time visualizing what we think, moving away from thinking into 'doing' and back again might help figure it out.

If you were to make a list of how you would want to be thinking about yourself, what would that list look like? Examine the short list below and provide any other wanted thoughts you can think of.

### Table 4 - Wanted Thoughts

| | | | |
|---|---|---|---|
| Attractive | Compassionate | Fun | Dependable |
| Loving | Strong | Kind | Calm |
| Content | Independent | Respect | Successful |
| Valued | Complete | Healthy | Peaceful |

Now, think about what you can do to start making changes in your thinking to get what you want.

In doing this, we concentrate on moving toward what we want, rather than away from what we don't. Take loneliness, for example. Rather than considering choices that might help us feel less lonely, we work on making choices that'll help change the way we think about ourselves. This could include reading, going out and doing fun things, or starting a long-procrastinated project or activity.

It's important to note that at this point, we should make sure the activity or activities we select are small enough to be accomplished. Again, this might be as simple as walking to the corner store, the bank or post office and, during the trip, making sure to smile and say "Hello" to everyone we meet.

## DOING

To begin this section of Dynamic Discovery, ask yourself, "What have I been doing that I really don't like doing?" or "What have I been doing that hasn't given me what I want?"

Because we've been working on thinking and feeling behaviors, we might be tempted to continue progressing in those terms. For example, if a person had a problem with getting angry, we would move from feeling to doing, like this:

> DD: *Is anger an action or a feeling?*
>
> Client: *It's a feeling.*
>
> DD: *What do you do when you get angry?*
>
> Client: *I yell a lot.*

From this simple example, we learn to sort out behaviors and separate our feelings from what we do and how we think.

Let's make a list of behaviors that we're currently doing and don't like. The list may include:

## Table 5 - Unwanted Behaviors

| | | | |
|---|---|---|---|
| Shouting | Arguing | Lying | Swearing |
| Violence | Abuse | Sicking | Depressing |
| Crying | Revenging | Blaming | Gossiping |
| Self-Pitying | Cheating | Drinking | Drugging |
| Snooping | Overeating | | |

As always, feel free to add your own 'doing' behaviors to this list, and cross out those that don't apply.

If you refer to the list and ask yourself, "Am I aware of the reasons behind my actions?" – you wouldn't be alone if you answered "Not really."

Although seemingly overwhelming, there's something to be said for acknowledging that oftentimes we don't know the reasons for our behaviors, and further acknowledging that these same behaviors have gotten us into an awful lot of trouble.

Remember, all of our behaviors relate back to the Control Theory and our five basic needs (LAFFS). These behaviors are our attempts at getting our needs met. Nothing short of death will ever stop us from trying to satisfy our five basic needs, even if the behaviors do not get us what we want.

To explain the effects that these actions have on other areas of our lives, let's use a client who got angry and yelled a lot as an example:

> DD: *How do you feel when you are shouting?*
>
> Client: *I feel really guilty.*
>
> DD: *What do you think about yourself when you are shouting?*
>
> Client: *I think that I'm not able to control myself very well.*
>
> DD: *How is that working out for you?*
>
> Client: *Not well.*
>
> DD: *Is it helping you get what you want?*
>
> Client: *No way.*
>
> DD: *What DO you want?*
>
> Client: *Well, like the others, I guess I want to be happy.*

Next, let's explore the controlling nature of these behaviors. Violence is almost always on the list. For example, we've all heard of situations when a physically abusive father stops beating his child when the child turns the table and physically abuses the father. As long as abusing his child appeared to be getting the father what he wanted, he continued to do it. When the table was turned, the price was too high for the abuse to continue. It seems that abusive behavior often stops when it no longer has any value to the person who is doing the behavior.

There are many examples in our society of people who have reformed, such as road-ragers, alcoholics and drug addicts. These people have literally decided that they've had enough of their old destructive behaviors because they were no longer getting their needs met through their addictions. They decided to change their behaviors in a way that would get them what they wanted – which, for the majority of people, is to be happy.

Would it surprise you to learn that many Dynamic Discovery participants believe that their own spouses, children or parents are victims of violent behavior? We are often quite surprised to learn that we ourselves use violence for a purpose, and that it's a controlled action. It's a good idea to take the time to go through the list of unwanted behaviors listed in Table 5, and know for certain that they are controlled and purposeful behaviors. While these purposeful behaviors may not be getting us what we want, they do get us something.

What can an abuser get out of beating someone up? The obvious answer is 'power' (as part of our need for Achievement, Power and Recognition). This is true in a lot of cases, but there is another benefit as well – and without this second benefit, the entire behavior is rendered useless.

Many of the 'doing' behaviors on the unwanted list will involve putting up barriers between the doer and other people. In the case of denial, it would mean the person is placing a barrier between themselves and the truth. Now ask yourself "Are my doing behaviors getting me what I want?"

Referring back to our list of things we'd rather not be doing in Table 5, is there behavior listed that you haven't done? Most, if not all, Dynamic Discovery participants will acknowledge that they've engaged in every single unwanted 'doing' behavior on the list.

Co-dependents have described using crying to control others; homemakers will admit to stealing; and abuse victims will tell of being abusers themselves. In short, it illustrates that this process levels the playing field among everyone undertaking the Dynamic Discovery process.

Instead of dwelling on past actions, we'll continue with the process of evaluation by asking ourselves, "If this is what you've been thinking and maybe doing and it hasn't been getting you what you want, what could you do that might get you what you want?"

If we then created a 'Want to be doing' list, what words would be on it?

### Table 6 - *Want To Be Doing*

| Accepting | Caring | Sharing | Strong |
|---|---|---|---|
| Smart | Courageous | Attractive | Loving |
| Open-minded | Peaceful | Volunteering | Trusting |

Note that not all the words on the list appear to be 'doing' behaviors. It seems that when we're asked what we don't want to be doing, like lying and shouting, we're very specific about our unwanted behaviors. Then when we're asked what we do want to be doing, we are much less specific. In addition, this want list contains 'feeling' and 'thinking' behaviors.

If someone was to ask you, for example, what 'honesty' looked like, what would you say? Difficult to answer, isn't it? The point is that we often have all kinds of ideas about how we want to be acting, but we have no idea what that behavior might look like.

Now it's important to take some time to try and visualize our 'want to be doing' behaviors and figure out what they would look like to us. Honesty is a great example because the 'telling the truth' component of honesty is extremely attainable and an action we can measure.

In group settings, an exercise that works well for Dynamic Discovery participants is to come up with a working list that may look like this:

### Table 7 - Working List

| Honest | Self- | Peaceful | Trustworthy |
|---|---|---|---|
| Open-minded | Accepting | Spiritual | Loving |
| Attractive | Confident | Compassionate | Assertive |

To dispel the vagueness in the list, go ahead and pick one of the words from the above list and ask yourself, "What would that look like to me?" We're so accustomed to dwelling on negatives that a new experience of focusing on exactly how these new and desired behaviors would look can be very exhilarating.

If you were being successful, what would you be doing, thinking and feeling? Or if you were being confident, what would confident look like to you?

## CONTROL CAR

Remember the Control Car theory – the way it establishes a link between what we think and how it affects our life? Any major elevation of our behaviors would have the same effect as greatly over-inflating a particular 'tire' and any repression of our behavior deflates a particular 'tire'. Either way, we'll end up feeling 'unbalanced'.

To review, these are the behaviors we've examined thus far in Dynamic Discovery:

> **DOING** – like drinking, worrying, violence and sicking.

> **THINKING** – like self-blame, self-pity and name-calling.

> **FEELING** – like depression, anger, fear and resentment.

The relationship of one behavior to another can be established by viewing our behavioral system as Dr. Glasser's front-wheel-drive Control Car.

## *Figure 6 - Control Car*

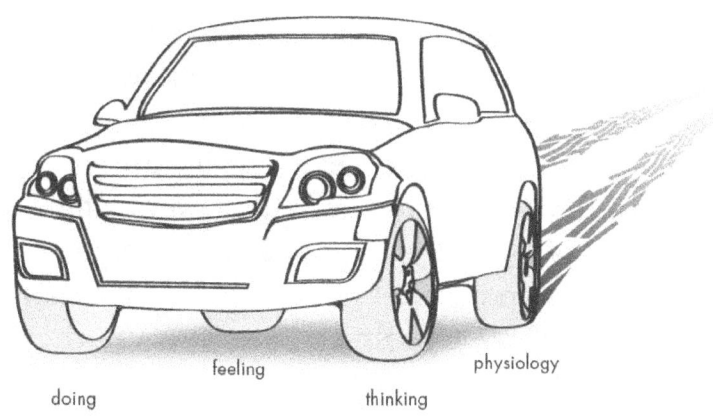

doing     feeling     thinking     physiology

Each behavior, by necessity, affects the other, but the thinking and doing behaviors dominate the others because they are both in the front end of this front-wheel-drive car. We are very much powered by our thinking and our doing behaviors and, in turn, what we do and think will most often control how we feel and our physiology.

At times, our doing and thinking behaviors will absolutely dictate an outcome. Drug use is a good example. The doing behavior of using a chemical to alter our feelings or thinking can have serious consequences on our entire behavioral system. Drinking to feel good affects what we do, think, feel, and our health.

But things like worrier's headaches, procrastination, or feelings of anxiety and stress are all psychological issues that people suffer from as a result of an unbalanced Control Car.

There are also people who spend a lot of time in their own head, trying to analyze their way out of dilemmas. We can refer to them as 'Overthinkers'. These are people who believe that if they could just figure out what to do, everything would be great. This type of person often has a personal library containing several self-help books. In one extreme case, a recent Dynamic Discovery participant identified more than 30 sources, counselors and workshops that she had tried in an attempt to recover from her unwanted behaviors. Not once did anyone ever suggest that she was over-analyzing herself. In this case, her Control Car looks like this:

## *Figure 7 - Overthinking Control Car*

This person stated that her constant thinking, analyzing and worrying behaviors resulted in an inability to function at any other level. She described herself as being a procrastinator, weak, useless, inept and unhealthy, with constant headaches. It was at this point in the process that she realized that her thinking wheel was so large that it was having an overpowering effect on all her other behaviors.

It's also important to note the cyclic nature of our behaviors. All of us are guilty of repeating old behaviors again and again, with the same results each time. Only when we're faced with the fact that our needs aren't getting met do we select a new behavior to try to meet those needs. If the behavior we choose is one that we have referred to as a 'negative' behavior, then the result will be that our needs will again go unmet. When we establish a new list of behaviors, a list that contains behaviors meaningful to us as individuals, then we'll begin to substitute these new behaviors for the old ineffective ones.

When one of these new behaviors meets our needs, we'll start using this new behavior again and again because of its positive result. Then, because of a positive outcome, we'll try yet another new behavior and, if that one works as well, then another new behavior will be repeated again and again. In the end, we will be left with new behaviors that will give us what we're really wanting.

By this time in the Dynamic Discovery process, we should know that what we were doing wasn't getting us what we wanted. Even those in denial will have to admit that their lives weren't perfect, that there are things they want and aren't getting.

A great example is someone who is on probation, looking for early release from jail. The probationer could be a repeat offender, involved in a cycle of the same negative or destructive behaviors. The probationer, by virtue of their participation, is already doing something to get what they wanted, by being open to looking at other options.

It's up to you to determine how and when you'll make the change from your old behaviors to your new ones, depending on your own life and circumstances.

For example, during one recent discussion in a Dynamic Discovery group session, a client noted that by repeating their old behaviors, they were in essence giving the keys to their life over to this behavior. These non-productive behaviors are blind drivers and know nothing of the individual's best interests.

In order for your car to properly drive you to where you really wanted to go, what would you be thinking, doing and feeling?

The final stage, and the vital portion of this section of Dynamic Discovery, is identifying the new behaviors that can and will get you what you want. By applying the knowledge we now have about the Control Car and how we can apply it to our unique circumstances, we understand that new behaviors are necessary in order to change the direction or functioning of our own Control Car. If we don't spend time identifying and implementing meaningful new behaviors, then all we've accomplished is educating ourselves more about our pain. Just know that in every circumstance, there are options to replace our old behaviors.

# How Relationships Are Affected By Behaviors

Now that we're proficient at self-evaluating our own behaviors, we can focus on evaluating our relationships.

Many people feel confusion when it comes to friendships, parental and/or spousal relationships, and many Dynamic Discovery participants start out blaming other people for their own difficulties – either entirely or partially.

*Figure 8 - Typical Relationship Chart*

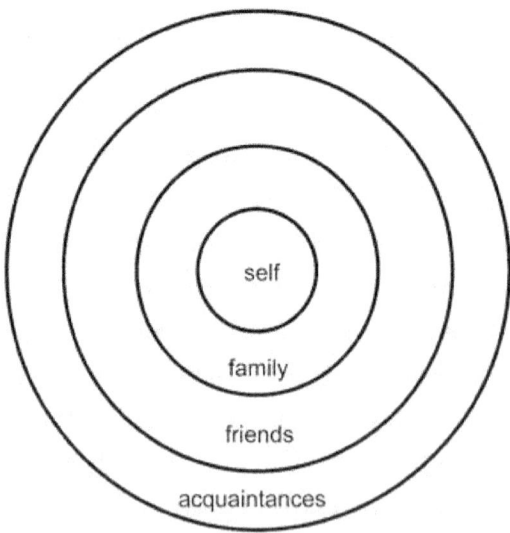

This chart is typical for most Dynamic Discovery participants. You are at the centre. Family members are typically the next closest, and then friends. It helps to illustrate the actual state of your relationships.

How have your unwanted behaviors as identified in Table 5 affected your relationships?

For example, as the illustration on the next page shows, an alcoholic might state that they feel removed from close relationships, have a sense of not fitting in or being disconnected from other people. From this illustration, we can safely assume that their 'doing' behavior of drinking is impacting their 'thinking' and 'feeling' behaviors. This person thinks and feels close to no one, and may very well be right. In this person's own mind, they are disconnected. In the past, they may have believed that the condition of these relationships was the cause of the drinking. But, through Dynamic Discovery, we know that the reverse is true; it's our behaviors that affect our relationships.

### *Figure 9 - How An Alcoholic's Needs Are Met*

We often think of how the behaviors of others affect us, but rarely about how our own behaviors affect our relationship with ourselves. Each of us has a very vital and important relationship with ourselves. To make sure it's a healthy one, we have to look at how our own behaviors affect our own lives by asking, "What have I been doing to me, and what impact has it had on my life?" and also "How have my behaviors erected barriers between me and other people in my life?"

Take a second, and think what it would be like if you always behaved in a way that would be in your own best interest. Remember, there is a difference between being selfish and acting in your own best interest. 'Best interest' is defined as "doing, thinking and feeling in ways which will help us get what we really want without causing harm to ourselves or others."

Undoubtedly, acting in our own best interest would inevitably lead us back to our 'wants', including: happiness, peace, health and serenity. On the other hand, acting out of selfishness regardless of the consequences, and especially if it causes ourselves or others harm, will never get us happiness, peace, health or serenity.

Co-dependent people often participate in Dynamic Discovery because of how others are affecting their lives. For example, when a co-dependent in a group session was asked where she was located on her own relationship map, she responded, "I'm blown completely off my own map." When she was asked to write her name on a piece of paper and place it somewhere in the room which would symbolize where she was in relation to her relationship map, she placed her name on the floor five feet away from her own chart.

This example illustrates just how far away we can be from acting in our own best interest, and also demonstrates how our own behaviors are the source of our own sense of remoteness.

Would it surprise you to know that a list of behaviors that support our own best interest and a list of wants would be virtually identical? It's true! And how convenient that all of the things we want are also all the things that are in our own best interest.

In our minds, we each have a concept of our own 'Ideal World'. This Ideal World would be what our world would be like if our wants were being satisfied and our needs were being met. We behave in ways that we believe will help us achieve and maintain our concept of an Ideal World. Now if you think of your Ideal World, what would that look like?

First, put yourself at the center of the map and work outwards with your relationships. An example of an Ideal World map might be similar to this:

### Figure 10 - Relationship Chart – Example 1

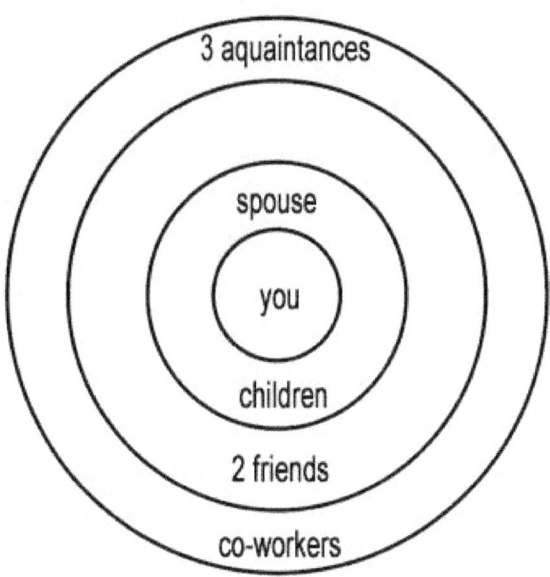

### Figure 11 - Relationship Chart – Example 2

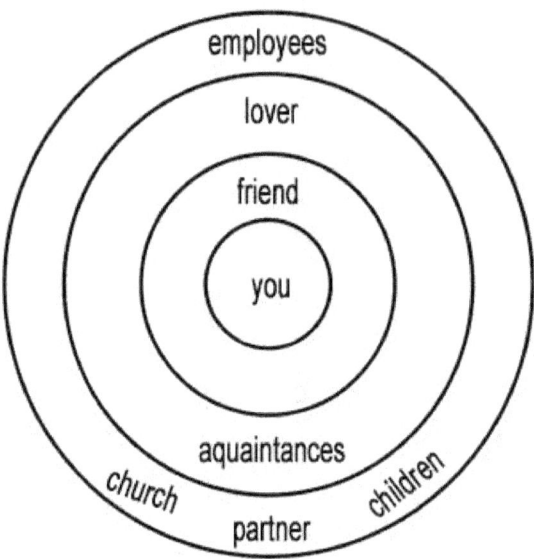

Now it's time to create your own relationship map. If you are at the centre of your universe, who is closest to you? And after them? And after them?

## *Figure 12 - Your Relationship Chart*

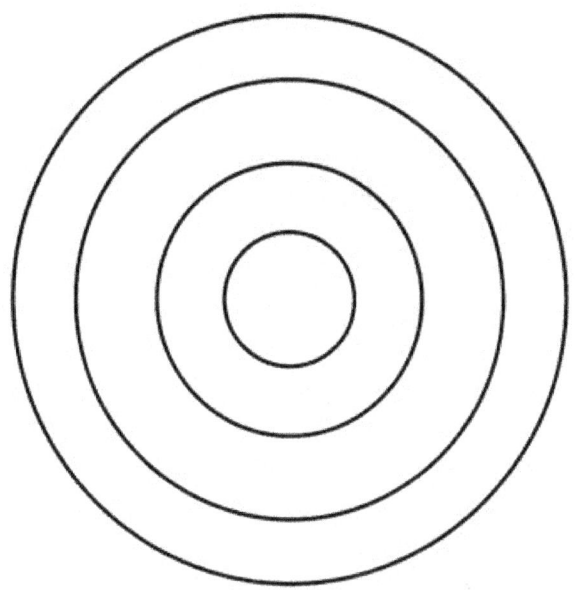

# Relationships As Affected By Needs

After completing your relationship chart in the previous chapter, you should have a clearer picture of the reality of your relationships with others. Now we'll look at how our relationships are meeting our five basic needs (LAFFS). To review, they are:

**Love and Belonging**

**Achievement, Power and Recognition**

**Freedom**

**Fun**

**Survival**

When we're not getting our wants and needs met, the result is to behave. In Dynamic Discovery terms, we cannot misbehave, because to do so would be to behave poorly, badly, or inappropriately. Knowing this helps us realize that no matter how ridiculous or nonsensical our behavior may be at times, it is merely a response to the drive we all have to try and get our needs met. No matter what we did, we were doing the best we knew how to do at the time. Isn't it a relief knowing that we don't have to make sense out of things that make no sense at all?

## *Figure 13 - Needs Chart*

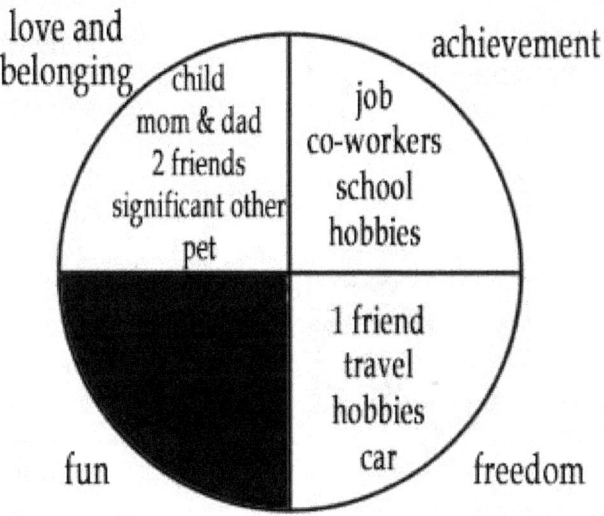

The preceding figure shows us what a typical Needs Chart looks like. Drawing this helps us to view relationships according to how they are or aren't meeting our needs. It's important to note that these relationships must be evaluated as they really are, rather than how they are supposed to be.

### Figure 14 - Your Needs Chart

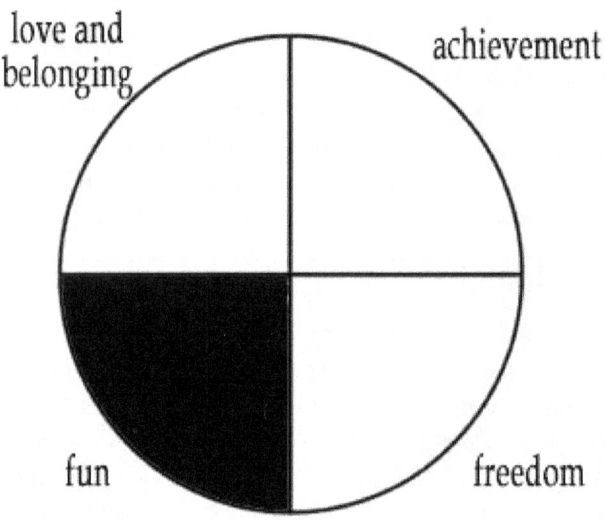

You might be tempted to draw your own diagram based on superficial appearances. Don't. If you're in a relationship in name only – with an estranged spouse, for instance – needs aren't being met in the relationship and it shouldn't be included on your chart.

In a Dynamic Discovery group session, a male participant described his relationship with a friend at work whom he felt was non-supportive and overly critical. When another friend told him that he always tried to surround himself with people who were supportive and positive, the participant said a light bulb came on because, he said, he hadn't realized that he had a choice as to who his friends were.

In Control Theory language, he had sought a co-worker's friendship to satisfy his need of Love and Belonging, but the relationship with his co-worker wasn't meeting that need. As a matter of fact, the relationship was making him feel less Love and Belonging than if he wasn't around his co-worker at all. Because they were thrown together at work, and because the co-worker was pleasant some of the time, he felt like he had no choice but to have a 'friendship'. Once he learned that it was in his own best interest to have and nurture relationships that met his needs, he sought them out. Although he continued to interact with his co-worker on a regular basis, he stopped viewing his relationship with his co-worker as a friendship, which left room to meet his need of Love and Belonging with others.

Let's now concentrate on evaluating how our behaviors have been working to meet our needs. A prime example is someone who uses food to fulfill their needs.

An overeater will evaluate their attempts to get their needs met by consuming food and drink as shown in the figure below:

## Figure 15 – Overeater's Needs Chart

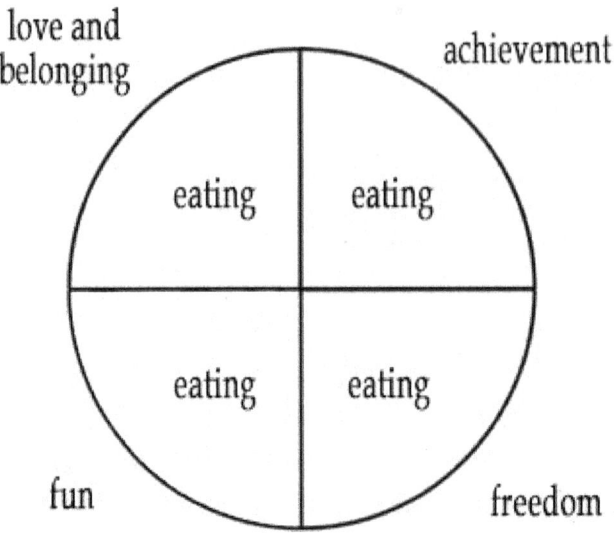

Overeaters claim they feel better, calmer, and more in control when they eat, and consuming food has been the only need-fulfilling behavior they've pursued in the past.

Any person with an obsession – which could include drinking, working, exercising – will draw a needs map very similar to the overeater's. Even the co-dependent will draw a map of how they have tried to get their needs met in the past with certain controlling actions, whether it is by trying to live someone else's life for them or by complying.

The next thing we'll do is examine how we're getting our needs met in our relationships. Since many of us have tried to get our needs met through obsessive behaviors, we shouldn't be surprised to learn that we're probably not getting our needs met through other people.

A great example of how we perceive our problems are with other people is to imagine being stuck in traffic, waiting to get out of a busy parking lot after a big event. While waiting in our cars in an endless line of traffic, at whom do we direct our anger? Usually we get mad at a person in another vehicle, not at the traffic planners, parking lot planners or event coordinators. Often, we perceive the root of the trouble to lie with the people involved. It could be spouses, friends, or acquaintances; only the circumstances vary.

## Figure 16 - How Relationships Meet Needs – Example 1

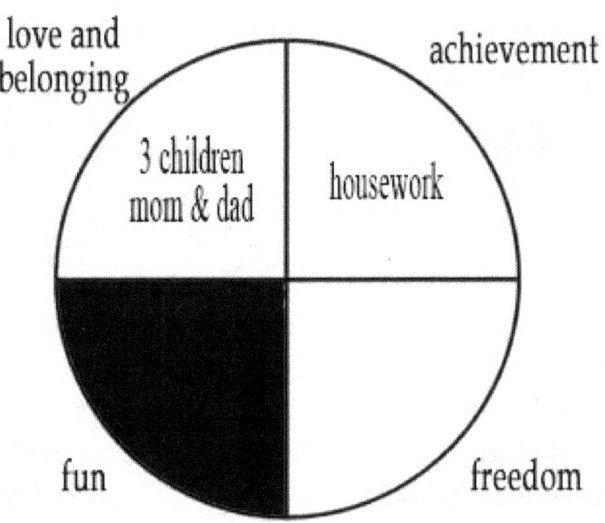

Regardless of your background or the reason you sought out Dynamic Discovery, the exercise you completed in Figure 14 reveals how the people in your life are either meeting your needs or not. When we talk about work or school, we tend to break those down into people or activities. In other words, if we perceive that we are getting our needs met at work, do we mean by our co-workers, or by our work itself? Or by both?

This helps us learn the important lesson of how to sort out how, or even if, a specific activity is meeting a need. One client who was heavily involved in their church saw the activity, but not the people, as need-fulfilling.

During these evaluations, Dynamic Discovery participants will often determine that several of their needs aren't being met. By going through these exercises one at a time, it emphasizes once again that we'll always behave in a way that we hope will get our needs met.

The next question we should ask ourselves is: "What do I think I've been doing to get my needs met?"

When you go through the process and evaluate your own behaviors from the perspective of "Well, I have to do something, don't I?" – the following questions may arise about the activities you undertake:

> *Have these activities been getting you what you want?*
>
> *Have they been working out for you?*
>
> *What do you think you could start doing instead?*

The following is an example of a single woman who loves her job, but hates her co-workers. Her Freedom needs are met through activities, not people.

### Figure 17 - How Relationships Meet Needs – Example 2

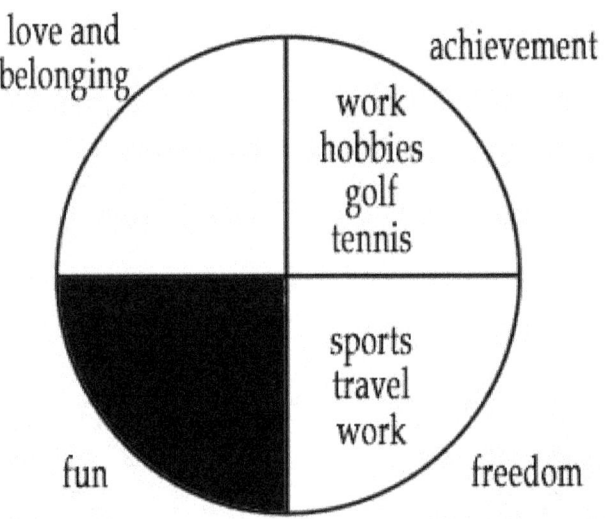

During a recent Dynamic Discovery group session, one participant stated they wanted to start getting their Love and Belonging need met at home with their parents. Up until then, they had viewed the breakdown of their relationship with their parents as "mostly their fault." During this exercise, they realized that if they wanted to meet their needs, they would have to take responsibility without heaping blame on their parents.

One way to do that was for our participant to commit to start telling their parents the truth instead of lies. We discussed what the truth would look like, and our participant decided that telling the truth 100% of the time wouldn't work. The suggestion of telling one or two truths didn't appeal to them either, as they felt that was too few. They decided on at least a dozen truths. After following through with their manageable actions, our participant reported back that their experience with their parents was "great."

This should now give you an idea of why you are or aren't comfortable with various situations or people in your life. If you can go forward evaluating your relationships, situations and activities on a 'needs met' basis, you'll be able to make some very vital decisions about how and with whom you spend your time.

For example, another recent Dynamic Discovery group session participant learned that one of her close relationships wasn't nearly as bad as she had previously thought. For years, she was under the impression that all she had to do was move out of her home and everything would be okay. After this exercise, she realized that what she really needed to do was to start meeting her Fun need and then she would start to feel better. It was relatively easy to find a way to start meeting that need, and without any terrible consequence to her family. Needless to say, her husband was relieved.

## SOLUTIONS

Dynamic Discovery is all about ending up with working solutions. Whether it is feeling better, thinking differently, or doing different things, the process always arrives at the new choices of solutions to obtain these wanted behaviors.

Since some of these solutions seem to be repetitive and might appear to be old answers, it is worth spending time on this subject. After all, arriving at solutions every day and sending people home with something they can actually do is the fundamental power in Dynamic Discovery.

It's a good idea to think about the solutions we want to find. We do this by empowering you to seek your own solutions, and therefore run your own life.

During yet another Dynamic Discovery group session, one participant came to the group due to a whole range of abuses. She was continually subjected to verbal, emotional and physical abuse at home. She readily recognized the physical abuse and understood that being strangled was an abusive act. As she progressed through the program, she became more and more aware of the other abuses she experienced. Being called stupid, useless and worthless were controlling behaviors that she soon realized were also abusive. One of the characteristics common to abused people is their old need to be told what to do. What she needed was some new way of dealing with the situation to make things better. And whatever that situation was to be, it had to lead to a win-win solution.

Again, there's immense value in starting new behaviors and not just changing old ones. This is because our new behaviors are designed to get us what we really want instead of getting rid of what we don't want.

> A win-win solution is one that:
>
> Addresses the need and not the want
>
> Is easily attainable
>
> Is tangible (a doing rather than a thinking)
>
> Is something the person wants to do
>
> Benefits the person, after doing it one time
>
> Meets a need, if the person continues doing it.

Choosing an activity that is reportable to another person is an added bonus, since the other person can help in marking your success. In addition, it is important to get a time frame in which this new activity will be done. Something to be accomplished at the end of the week may be too distant in time, especially for people who tend to procrastinate.

Once again, we refer to our five basic needs:

> Love and Belonging
>
> Achievement, Power and Recognition
>
> Freedom
>
> Fun
>
> Survival

It's imperative to remember that what we've done in the past or even what we're doing now doesn't need to make sense. It's easily explained by doing the following exercise:

Think of one day in your life where, given the information you had at the time, you did not do your best. Are you thinking, "But I should have known …" or "I should have thought …", or "I should have done …"?

If you had known, would it have made a difference in what you'd do? And knowing what you know now, would you do things differently if that situation arose again?

The point is, behaviors don't have to make sense and from now on, you can be free from the trap of spending precious energy trying to make sense out of nonsense. This idea sheds light on the uselessness of guilt.

Speaking of guilt...

Everyone wants to hang onto theirs. Not only do we want to hang onto it, we insist we need to keep it, even as we're trying to get rid of it!

A great example is of a Dynamic Discovery participant who had great success in her work, but not in her relationships. She had married and divorced two times and had a son who was a recovering addict. On top of that, she had a mother whom she could not keep happy. The very thing that she held closest to her was her ongoing guilt about her life. She maintained that if she had only been a better wife, daughter and mother, that all these people would have been happier. The desire to become a 'better' person was her motivation to join the group.

> DD: *How is all this guilt working out for you?*
>
> Client: *I don't like the feeling, but it is helping me out.*
>
> DD: *What kind of benefits are you getting from your guilt?*
>
> Client: *It helps me stop doing the bad things I was doing.*

Let that sink in ...

She said, "It helps me stop doing the bad things I was doing," yet even though she held onto her guilt, she continued to do those things she referred to as "bad" – entering and leaving intimate relationships and proclaiming responsibility for the inappropriate behaviors of others.

Does anyone need guilt to motivate change? No. And all of us who cling to guilt would serve ourselves well to make a decision about our actual need for guilt.

Let's deal our guilt a crushing blow by asking ourselves exactly who benefits from feeling guilt. Hint: it's not us. Guilt only serves others, and being guilty is never acting in our own best interest. Furthermore, guilt is a tactic other people use in an attempt to keep the guilty party 'in line'. Guilt rears its ugly head on a regular basis and it always bears attending to, since most people who use guilt as a controlling behavior insist on holding onto it.

Letting go of pointless guilt and committing to win-win solutions is a logical next step.

But how do we arrive at win-win solutions on a daily basis? One guideline to follow is to keep all solutions to the level of manageability. We tend to want too much and all at once, when it would be in our own best interests to keep the solutions manageable and within sight.

And, we can identify what need (or needs) we're controlling through an exercise we refer to as Fantasy – which is an imagined or conjured-up sequence fulfilling a psychological need, or a daydream.

In Dynamic Discovery group sessions, participants are asked to write down their Fantasy on a piece of paper and – whether it be moving to a Caribbean island or quitting their job to pursue a life with the Peace Corps – to elaborate on what they would be thinking, feeling and doing in that new life.

One participant had a dream of living on the coast, with no money worries and no responsibilities, and having time to dust off her easel, canvas and paints so as to begin the creative process she gave up when her life became overly busy and complicated. And unhappy. Oh, and while she was serving her artistic nature, she was awaiting the return of her special fella… because she was alone and lonely.

When she read her Fantasy to the group, it was easy to see what her win-win solutions could be – the only decision for her to make involved identifying which to start on first – but she identified that her problem would be to find the time to be creative and meet potential love interests. The feedback from the leader and the rest of the group was really only a reminder that she did not have to instantly create a masterpiece or immediately meet, court and marry the love of her life. The goal of the win-win solutions is to get started on serving the need. The conclusion reached was that upon arriving home that day, that she would do an inventory of her painting supplies. Any missing pieces would be bought the next day and the day after that, she would set up her easel and canvas so that, on the following day, she could set aside 30 minutes and make a start on a sketch or drawing.

In order to get a start on meeting available men, she agreed that going out with friends to do actual fun and interesting things might well work since people enjoying themselves is attractive. She also agreed that available men attended church, shopped for food and... well, every other thing that available women do.

Finally, we asked her to be aware that it was important to stop obsessing over finding an intimate partner as she was probably walking right by the person who could be a partner or a great friend. The reason for this is that the people who become special to us seldom look the way we see them in our minds.

The group discussed the fact that a huge part of our attractiveness is our attitude. As examples of that, we identified men and women in the public eye who would not be considered handsome or beautiful but are, nonetheless, considered attractive because of their demeanor and attitude. Simply put, being attractive is more than just a look – it's a frame of mind that allows you to act and project a confident, sexy, and intriguing look. Whether you're just walking down the street or stopping to have a quick conversation, if you go about it the right way, everyone in your orbit will be thinking of you as a very attractive person in no time.

Another woman's Fantasy had her walking on a Caribbean beach every day and writing for a living. She had originally claimed to be unwanted, unloved and lonely, but by her own evaluation, she stated that her prevailing need appeared to be for Freedom. This is not to say that she didn't have a need for Love and Belonging, but her need for Freedom was more pressing and felt an immense relief to be able to start working towards Freedom instead of away from loneliness.

Another Dynamic Discovery group session participant was the victim of abuse at the hands of her husband. Obviously, leaving home was a choice she could make, but she couldn't see herself doing that. She said she had tried unsuccessfully to leave on a prior occasion and failed because she had no support. The support she required meant she had to make contacts in the community, so she wasn't solely reliant on the old abusive situation to get all her needs met.

Through self-evaluation, she decided that returning to teaching adults to read was a solid choice and she decided to go for it. She made a commitment to

make inquiries about the local adult tutoring centre that very day and said she would report back to the group at the next session.

She was taking steps to gain independence through this new rewarding activity. The task of leaving held too many possibilities for losing, and if she stayed without making any changes, she would be remaining in a totally losing situation. She wanted to start gaining, and her choice to garner support and defer making a final decision about leaving was an effective choice for her.

In the end, because of her new choices, she did leave her abusive home. In order for her to get to that point, she had to start getting her needs met in manageable ways. Then she was able to re-evaluate and decide whether she wanted to make the big move, and it turned out to be her win-win solution.

The solutions presented above might not seem like such a big deal in relation to the underlying problems, but they're totally effective when measured against the potential for success.

The entire Dynamic Discovery process is geared toward one thing; the success and recovery of our participants. It also shows that success can be, and is, both possible and manageable.

## CONCLUSION

Now that you've read Dynamic Discovery, please remember that recovery is a process, not necessarily a single event. Recovery is a way of living, a quality of feeling, and a mental attitude. Because you are reading this, you've likely started the recovery process, which probably began with the realization, or just a suspicion, that your life was not progressing in a way that was healthy.

The knowing or suspicion that something was amiss was likely what drew you to Dynamic Discovery – and that was enough for the recovery process to start. Letting go of the pain and fear is a necessary part of the recovery process, and as we let go, happiness, freedom and joy become a way of life rather than just words spoken or read. I have seen this happen again and again. Joy and love of life are the rewards for walking through the 'pain' of growth.

Just as a map is not the territory but a guide to the territory, I hope that this book will prove to be a map to the territory of 'self'.

The amount of happiness that is available to you as you continue to apply your newfound skills and techniques is infinite, because you define the goal at the top by the power of your increasing vision; the higher you climb, the farther you can see. And when you stop and rest and enjoy the view from your new vantage point, there is nothing sweeter.

There is no limit to the passion and meaning that you can derive from your journey. You can incorporate any existing tool or program within the larger context of this journey – as long as it makes you more powerful, awake and responsible. And that is your pathway to freedom.

Because your path is right there for you, it's important to remember that, no matter what happens, the path that you created is right before you – all you have to do is walk the path, and you will feel the power of your design.

When I think of the wasted dreams, the unfulfilled lives and the lost opportunities in so many of the people around me, I feel sad... sad and more committed than ever to disseminating Dynamic Discovery material through our website and the included blog posts (www.dynamicdiscovery.ca). But I don't see this program as a completed product; I see Dynamic Discovery as something that can continue to evolve so as to enable us to work with people suffering from shattering problems such as Post Traumatic Stress Disorder.

To remind you of the value of keeping an open mind, I have provided the familiar images of two straight lines (of equal length) and a candlestick (or two faces) to illustrate that things are often not as they first seem, and there's almost always a different perspective.

### *Figure 18 and Figure 19 - Perspective*

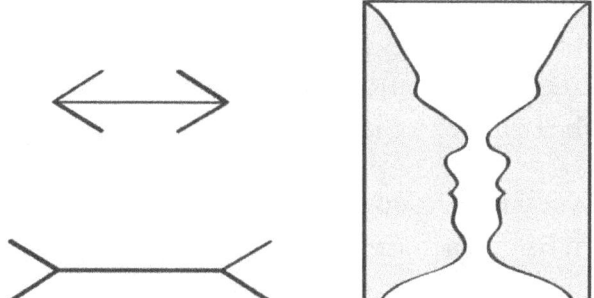

So it's the same principle with everything – each situation, event, conversation means something different to all those involved, and to those not involved. We give different meanings, according to our belief systems, and how we are affected by the event. We all have our own realities.

Finally, in case I was not clear about myself, let me now clarify some things:

I do not consider myself to be an 'expert' on human behavior nor any kind of 'guru' in the therapy world.

I do not think that I am super-intelligent, but I do know that I am intelligent – like everyone else who has been schooled, either formally or self-taught. How could one prosper in our world today if one was mentally deficient? Remember, though, intelligent people can act stupid – where the term 'stupid' means lacking intelligence or common sense – when convinced by an authority figure that they are stupid.

My knowledge and beliefs concerning human behavior came about over the course of many years of working with people who sought my assistance to deal with a rather long list of personal problems.

The Dynamic Discovery program is not about advice, it is about helping you find your way to a better life... as you determine it. By the way, if advice was all we needed to build a better life, then all one would have to do is just stand on any street corner and, within time, you would be overwhelmed with advice. I believe this: advice by itself could provide the perfect answer, but the reason why it is not enough is because the advice we receive seldom contains a detailed description of how to implement it.

Remember, we do not evaluate for right and wrong, or for good and bad. What is is, and what ain't ain't.

You can't be measured by someone else's yardstick.

If you want to know more, go to our website (www.dynamicdiscovery.ca), where you will find information about the Dynamic Discovery Workbook.

www.ingramcontent.com/pod-product-compliance
Lightning Source LLC
Chambersburg PA
CBHW060511030426
42337CB00015B/1846